GARDEN CONSTRUCTION

*Created and designed
by the editorial staff
of ORTHO Books*

Project Editor
Jim Beley

Writer
T. Jeff Williams

Illustrators
Ron Hildebrand
Ronda Hildebrand

Ortho Books

Publisher
Robert L. Iacopi

Editorial Director
Min S. Yee

Managing Editors
Anne Coolman
Michael D. Smith
Sally W. Smith

Production Manager
Ernie S. Tasaki

Editors
Jim Beley
Susan Lammers
Deni Stein

System Manager
Christopher Banks

System Consultant
Mark Zielinski

Asst. System Managers
Linda Bouchard
William F. Yusavage

Photographic Director
Alan Copeland

Photographers
Laurie A. Black
Richard A. Christman

Asst. Production Manager
Darcie S. Furlan

Associate Editors
Richard H. Bond
Alice E. Mace

Production Editors
Don Mosley
Kate O'Keeffe

Chief Copy Editor
Rebecca Pepper

Photo Editors
Anne Pederson
Pam Peirce

National Sales Manager
Garry P. Wellman

Sales Associate
Susan B. Boyle

Operations Director
William T. Pletcher

Operations Assistant
Gail L. Davis

Administrative Assistant
Georgiann Wright

Address all inquiries to
Ortho Books
Chevron Chemical Company
Consumer Products Division
575 Market Street
San Francisco, CA 94105

Copyright © 1985
Chevron Chemical Company
All rights reserved under
international and Pan-American
copyright conventions.

First Printing in March, 1985

3 4 5 6 7 8 9
86 87 88 89 90

ISBN 0-89721-046-8 UPC 05907

Library of Congress Catalog Card
Number 85-060004

Acknowledgments

Graphic Design
Jonson Pedersen Hinrichs & Shakery
San Francisco, CA

Photographers
William Aplin: p. 30, 32, 38 (middle, right), 41
  (middle center, bottom middle), 52 (bottom), 61
  (top, middle), 74, 76, 91, 92 (bottom)
Martha Baker: p. 1, 19 (left), 57 (bottom)
Carol Bernson: p. 51
Dennis Bettencourt: p. 15, 92 (top)
Laurie Black: p. 20 (bottom), 21 (bottom), 43 (bot-
  tom), 52 (top), 54, 56 (top), 64 (bottom), 65
  (bottom), 88 (bottom)
John Blaustein: p. 8 (left), 9 (bottom), 12
Ernest Braun, California Redwood Association: p.
  31 (top)
Josephine Coatsworth: p. 13, 33 (top, bottom), 70
  (bottom), 93 (left)
Richard A. Christman: p. 34, 41 (top middle), 49
  (top), 57 (top), 86
Alan Copeland: p. 40 (top), 49 (middle)
Rufus Diamant, California Redwood Association: p.
  40 (bottom)
Derek Fell: p. 53
Barbara Ferguson: p. 64 (top)
Barry M. Friesen: p. 7 (top), 37
Tony Howarth: p. 71
Susan Lammers: p. 21 (top), 42 (top), 46, 47, 49
  (bottom)
Fred Lyon: p. 27 (top)
Michael Landis: Back Cover (top right, bottom
  right), p. 3, 4 5, 6 (top, bottom), 8 (middle),
  16 17, 18 (top), 22, 26 (top, bottom), 27 (bot-
  tom), 35, 38 (left), 42 (bottom), 50 (bottom), 55
  (top), 56 (middle, bottom), 68 (top right, bottom),
  69, 70 (top), 72 73, 80
Michael McKinley: p. 7 (bottom), 10, 18 (bottom),
  23, 31 (bottom), 41 (middle right, bottom left), 48
  (right), 55 (bottom), 60, 93 (right)
J. McNair: p. 8 (right), 31 (middle), 41 (top right)
Ortho Photo Library: Back Cover (bottom left), p.
  36, 41 (bottom right), 45, 59, 61 (bottom), 62, 68
  (top left), 88 (top)
Anne Pederson: p. 65 (top)
Karl Riek, California Redwood Association: p. 48
  (left)
Tom Tracy: p. 9 (top), 20 (top), 24, 25, 39, 50 (top)
T. Jeff Williams: p. 19 (right)
Jeff Wasserman, California Redwood Association:
  p. 41 (top left), 43 (top)
William H. Wilson: p. 41 (middle left)

Front Cover:
The patio, shade structure, retaining walls, and rustic
path make this yard a special place to relax or
entertain friends.

Back Cover:
Upper left: This patio and shade structure create an
outdoor room for summer activities.

Upper right: The addition of outdoor lighting makes
this deck useable at night as well as in the daytime.

Bottom left: This wood walk adds a sense of drama
to this wood lot.

Bottom right: A compost bin is a useful and easy-to-
build project.

Title Page:
A shade stucture can add a distinctive touch to an
otherwise common patio or deck.

Landscape Designers
Kirk Aiken: p. 36 (bottom)
Bennett Christoferson: p. 40 (bottom)
Roger Fiske: p. 56 (top)
Michael Thomas Issel: p. 49 (middle)
Chris Pattilo, ASLA: p. 7 (top)
Barry M. Friesen: p. 37

Consultant
Jerry Craig
Blue Ridge, VA

Special Thanks to:
Mary Lou Carlson
Teresa Castle
Eric Claussen
Charlene Draheim
Toshio Mitsuda
Loretta & Robin Taylor

Chevron Chemical Company
575 Market Street, San Francisco, CA 94105

GARDEN CONSTRUCTION

DESIGNING AND PLANNING YOUR PROJECT

This book will do more than give you ideas for garden projects like a deck, pathway, or wall—it will show you how to improve the overall appearance of your property. In the following pages, you will find ideas for all the projects you want to build in your yard, along with the practical information you need to turn those ideas into reality.

To bring about a significant change in your property, the type that makes people stop and take a breath in appreciation, you will want to consider your property as a single entity. To help you, the first section of the book presents a detailed approach to the principles of yard design—the same concepts that a landscape architect would use in designing or redesigning your yard.

The second section, Garden Projects, presents an array of ideas that you can use in planning improvements of your property. This section shows you patios, decks, walks, stairs, fences, gates, walls, shade structures, storage areas, raised planting beds, and more.

In the third section, Construction Techniques, you'll also find details on the special techniques and tricks of working with wood, brick, stone, and concrete: the most common elements in garden construction. Included are specifics on what to look for when ordering lumber and the types of tools needed for wood construction projects.

This outdoor design brings together all the elements of the yard, from house to patio to garden and trees, into a balanced statement. The design features basic design principles: a unique-shaped patio, a combination of materials, and multiple levels.

THE DESIGN PROCESS

There is a difference between design and decoration. When you plant a few flowers and shrubs, hoping they will improve the appearance of your yard, that is decoration.

Design is the process of bringing together all the elements of the yard, from house to patio to garden and trees, into a balanced statement.

Getting Started

A successful landscape reflects your own desires, your own dreams. So the successful design starts with you. Think about beautiful places you have seen in your life, places that brought you a sense of beauty and harmony. This could be any scene, from a sunlit glen in the forest to your grandmother's vegetable garden.

Start by building a scrapbook of ideas. Anytime you see a magazine photograph of a garden or yard that appeals to you, tear it out and save it. Drive around your neighborhood, looking for gardens and yards that you like, and make notes on them. Take photographs of landscapes you particularly enjoy.

In planning your landscape, keep in mind that you may actually have a public and a private yard. The public yard is frequently the front yard, and the private one is the backyard. Even the front yard may be made semiprivate through judicious plantings of shrubs and trees.

Another technique to keep in mind in landscape planning is the use of the "borrowed landscape," in which the surrounding vistas are seen as an extension of your yard. The trick here is to let the eye naturally settle on the boundary limits of your yard through the use of a low fence or low moundings of earth planted with a ground cover or flowers.

Top: *As you design your yard and garden, it is helpful to think of your yard in terms of a bird's eye view.*

Bottom: *This view incorporates the vista beyond the low hedge to make this deck seem more spacious.*

A final consideration in general landscape planning is the incorporation of the natural terrain of your area into your own yard. This means designing the yard with an eye to your climate, whether arid or humid, and to the lay of the land, whether mountainous or flat. Use plants and building materials that harmonize with your area rather than conflict with it.

Design Principles

Following some of the general principles of landscape design will help you create a successful yard or landscape. The following pages take you into the specifics of three key design elements: perspective, form, and appeal to the senses.

Perspective

In planning your grounds, consider the primary perspective from which they will be viewed. The angle from which your yard is commonly seen helps determine its impact on the viewer: a yard seen from a high vantage point gives the viewer a sense of command, one seen from a level point makes the viewer feel directly connected to the vista, while a yard seen from a lower level may give the viewer either a sense of security or the feeling of being confined. A deck or patio, for instance, can be placed on a natural or created hillock in your yard to provide a commanding perspective, while a pathway leading from a ground-floor doorway to the garden will link the eye directly with the garden.

The imaginary line formed as your eyes naturally come to rest on a tree or flower bed, for instance, is termed the "axis of the landscape." In a formal garden, this axis is arranged in straight or geometric lines that direct the eyes to focus toward some prize object at the far reaches of the garden, such as a flowering shrub or a fountain. In an informal garden, the eyes are also led to a specific area but with more subtlety. A gently curving walk may direct the view to a wildflower garden, for instance.

Top: *This deck extends over the slope to provide drama as well as added space.*

Bottom: *The brick walk forms an axis that helps focus attention on the fountain at the far end of the landscape.*

Effective landscape planning incorporates a sense of mystery in the perspective, rather than displaying every feature of the yard at once. But the view must suggest a solution to the mystery. A curved pathway that disappears behind a solid hedge may suggest entrapment to some people. This can be easily corrected by pruning the hedge enough to suggest openness on the other side.

Your sense of perspective is influenced by an awareness of what is in the foreground, the middle ground, and the background. Planting a large tree in the foreground and a smaller one in the background will make the yard seem longer than it actually is; reversing the two trees will make a long yard seem more compact than it is. This technique is known as "forcing the perspective."

In considering the different perspectives of a garden, remember also how they are to be connected. A focal point should be joined with the whole through the paths, patios, boardwalks, or stepping stones.

Form

The eyes are so constantly bombarded with forms that the brain filters out most of them; only when a form is set apart does it readily become apparent. Too many forms can make the yard appear cluttered; too many contrasting forms—curves struggling against straight lines—can give you a sense of unease.

Shrubs and flowers can be planted to match the curves, angles, or straight lines in your garden plan. When laying out walls or walkways, you can break up the monotony of repeated straight lines by adding curves or angles. When planning angles, try to maintain a certain continuity, by using 30-, 60-, and 90-degree angles, or 45- and 90-degree bends.

The symbolism that forms evoke must also be considered when you are drawing up your landscaping plans. Curves evoke feelings of harmony, as epitomized by the ancient Chinese form showing the "yin" and "yang" principles, which are opposites, such as light and darkness or strength and weakness, that balance each other. Circular forms also provide a sense of security. If your yard is on top of a leveled hill with an expansive view, a low wall along the property edge will bring the eye to rest there and give the viewer a bearing in the surrounding vista.

Tall objects, such as a line of poplars or a steeply terraced bank behind your house, evoke a sense of awe. On the other end of the scale, diminutive forms induce curiosity. Examples of such forms could be anything from a miniature garden to leaf patterns pressed into a concrete walk

Form can also suggest power. Consider a rugged rock formation projecting from the earth in the midst of a carefully tended lawn: the contrast of the rough rock to the manicured setting provides excitement in the landscape. A cantilevered deck that projects over a slope, seeming to defy gravity, provides a sense of power that can add a little magic to an otherwise routine setting.

These angled steps form a clean, simple transition between deck and lawn.

The contrast of materials in this landscape creates a sense of drama in this front yard.

Plant variety offers a strong foreground, middle ground, and background.

Senses

Along with perspective and a balance of forms, you should strive to incorporate in the landscape the third essential part of design: an appeal to the senses. Our senses respond to light, sound, temperature, touch, and fragrance, all of which directly influence our enjoyment of a yard.

An awareness of the senses during design work can forestall future problems, such as noise. If street noises are bothersome in your area and codes forbid high fences, a hedge or row of dense conifers will help to block out sound.

Of course, good design heightens a landscape's appeal to the sense of sight: a drab concrete walkway can be revitalized by covering it with brick; if that is too much work, an extra wide border of bright flowers planted along the path, will also add visual excitement.

In planning the location of a patio, you will need to be aware of the climate's effect on the senses. If you live in an area of hot summers, for instance, you may want to locate your patio in protective shade. You also need to be aware of the prevailing winds. If the house itself will not screen the wind from the patio, you might plan a decorative wood fence, a concrete block wall, or a hedge.

One aspect of the landscape that has a great appeal to the senses is texture. Contrasting textures evoke a sense of peace and tension at the same time, just as the contrasting principles of yin and yang form a unified whole. The textures in your garden can range from a smooth redwood deck to a thick layer of decorative bark that flanks a flower garden. Another example of contrasting yet balanced textures can be found in delicate flowers growing next to rugged stones along a path.

Colors in the garden also make a distinct statement, and can affect the mood of your property. A yard designed around numerous shade trees may project a sense of serenity, or it may simply appear drab; a sprinkling of brightly colored flower beds or flowering shrubs can add sparkle to the landscape. Colors can also alter the apparent size of a yard. Pastels make a space seem larger than it is, while brighter hues are more dominant and diminish the sense of space.

Blues and grays make forms appear to recede into the distance. Thus, a long, narrow lot can be made to appear wider by placing rows of pastel or pale blue flowers along its edges, and the end of the lot can be brought closer to the eye with brightly colored plantings.

Top: *The contrasting textures of plants, rocks, and wood along this walk stimulate one's senses.*

Bottom: *These colorful flowers and shrubs add sparkle to this landscape.*

LAYOUT PROCEDURES

Planning your garden means first putting your ideas on paper. Faced with the prospect of laying out a garden, many people go out into the yard and say, "A hyacinth over there might look nice, and how about a barbecue here."

But the result is likely to be as haphazard as the planning process. To construct a unified plan, you first need to put on paper all the elements on your property, from the house to the trees, fences, and walkways, and then start playing with ideas.

The Base Plan

The first step in landscaping is to make the base plan, which is an accurate record of what now exists on your property. Using the 100-foot tape, measure the perimeter of your property and the distance from the sides of your house to the property lines, then accurately draw your house and property lines on the graph paper. Now measure and draw on your base plan all the other significant features of your property. These should include the doors and windows of the house, the location of outside faucets, the circular outline of trees, the driveway and paths around your house, and the location of any underground utilities.

Now take the rough sketch of the base plan and draw it again on a fresh sheet of graph paper, this time making it neat and using the templates and architect's scale to accurately draw all the elements in the yard. At the top left of the base plan, note the direction of north so the plan can always be oriented correctly.

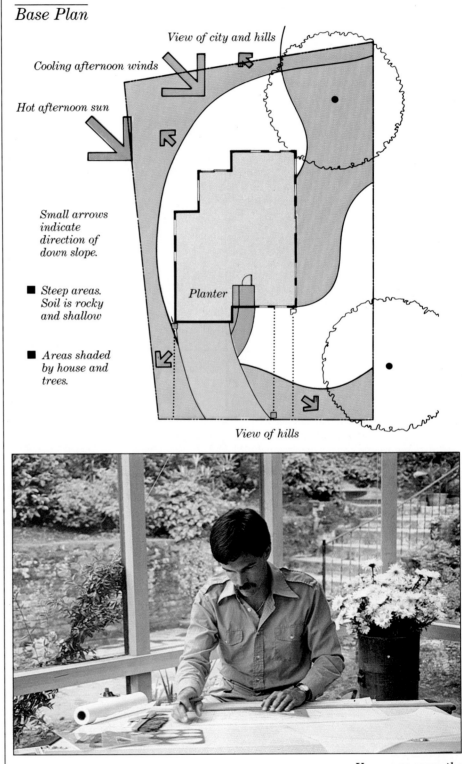

Base Plan

View of city and hills

Cooling afternoon winds

Hot afternoon sun

Small arrows indicate direction of down slope.

■ Steep areas. Soil is rocky and shallow

Planter

■ Areas shaded by house and trees.

View of hills

You can prepare the drawings with inexpensive drafting tools available from any office supply store.

Also indicate with arrows where the good views are, and where the views are less than desirable. Three other items that are important to note on the base plan are prevailing winds, shadow patterns that may affect your design, and low spots that collect water in the wet season.

With the base plan done, you are ready to start creating a new design for your yard.

Working Plans

The working plans are divided into two stages: the bubble plan and the concept drawing. This is the stage when you start putting ideas down on paper to see how they look, then making changes as better ideas and solutions come to mind.

The Bubble Plan

The bubble plan is largely an exercise in imagination. It consists of nothing more than rough circles, or bubbles, sketched on a piece of tracing paper laid over the base plan. Draw circles and ellipses of what you would dream about in a new landscape: a big circle for a deck jutting out from the house, a smaller circle for a reflecting pool, a long curving circle in the back yard for a flower garden. If something doesn't work, use a fresh sheet of tracing paper and start over.

Once you begin to see a clear picture of the landscape, start to make your bubble plan a little more specific. Sketch in how you want one space to relate to another; show the circulation patterns, such as paths or walkways; detail how you will take advantage of views with patios, decks, or sitting areas.

The Concept Drawing

The concept drawing follows from the bubble plan, and distills its generalizations down to specifics. With a fresh sheet of tracing paper over the base plan, transfer the ideas generated in the bubble plan to scale drawings. Feel free to modify your earlier concepts; there is always more than one way to landscape a yard.

In the concept drawing, consider how the landscape will be seen from inside the house and from the street, the sun angles, views, noise, and winds. Consider all your design options. You may want to change levels of decks or patios, for instance, or add a rocky outcropping.

Working Drawings

Now you are ready to make the working drawings you will use when you actually start construction. These are similar to the concept drawings, only much more detailed. For instance, if you are planning a deck, at this stage you will draw the deck from the footings to the railings, with all the dimensions carefully stated. These drawings can be turned into blueprints for the local building inspector and for contractors or workers, if necessary. (Look in the Yellow Pages for blueprint services.)

Your working drawings should show the layout of the grounds in precise detail, with pathways drawn to scale, brick or wood patterns indicated where necessary, and the type and size of trees and shrubs.

At this point, you may feel like starting right in on your project, but remember: good plans are half the battle. Be sure your plans show the landscape and all the new features just the way you want them to look. Only then are you ready to start making your paper plans real.

Working Drawing

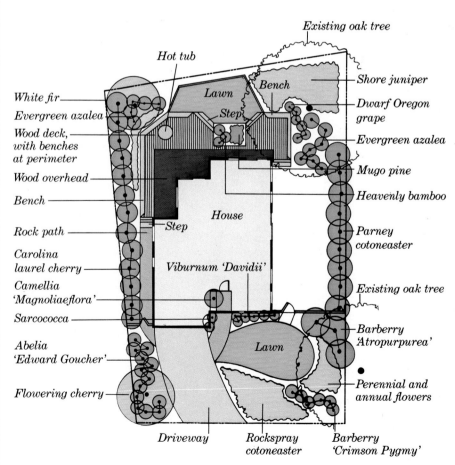

CONSTRUCTION PLANNING

*A*lthough this book is aimed at those who want to do the work themselves, everyone has limits. Should you hire a contractor to do all or part of the work? Here are some considerations to help in making the decision.

Because of their training and experience, landscape architects can prove helpful in designing your property. They know how to put all the elements together in a pleasing and eye-catching manner. Naturally, however, they tend to lean toward what they like and think is best for the property, and you may find that your views come in second.

You will be better able to determine if you need the services of a landscape architect if you first do all the preliminary work described earlier. Measure your grounds and make the base plan, then continue on to the bubble plan and concept drawing until you have a good idea of what you want on your property.

At some point, you may draw a blank. Something may not quite fit or blend with the whole the way you know it could, and you may not be able to find the solution. This is when you should go to a landscape architect—or rather he or she should come to your place—for an injection of ideas. Because you have done all your homework and have a firm grasp of the basic plan, it shouldn't take the architect long to provide a number of solutions, one of which will prove ideal for your yard.

How do you go about finding a good landscape architect? Word-of-mouth recommendations from friends and neighbors are always a mark of high praise. You can also call two or three landscape architects in your community and discuss your situation on the phone. Their response to your questions will be an indication of how well they might work with you. And don't be shy about asking how much they charge. If your budget is limited, you might try contacting the landscape architecture department at the nearest college or university and arrange to have one of the students there work with you.

When it comes to doing the physical work involved in landscaping your yard, you can do it all yourself, hire helpers, or contract it all out. A landscape architect is a good source of recommendations for contractors.

Since there are no fixed prices in contract work, you should ask at least three different contractors to visit your property and give you a written bid. The bid should include specific information, such as the size and quality of pipe to be laid for sprinkler systems, the quantity of pressure treated lumber, or the type of brick to be used in a patio.

Once you select a contractor, request a written contract that specifies the work to be done, the materials to be used, and a completion date.

Specify the quality of each material required to prevent the contractor from substituting lesser quality at a much lower cost.

On smaller jobs, some contractors may stop in the middle of a job when a bigger and more lucrative offer comes along. Write into the contract a per-day penalty clause for work uncompleted. Contractors are licensed, and if contract disputes arise, the matter can be taken to the state licensing board.

The contract should also specify the payment schedule. You will normally pay about one-fourth of the total as a down payment, with the remainder to be paid as specified amounts of work are completed. However, agree in advance that the final portion will not be paid until at least two weeks after all work has been completed. This is done because a contractor may hire other workers for the job and then, for various reasons, not pay them. Those unpaid workers can file a lien against your property, which you must pay before you can sell your property. Any such problem should surface during the two-week waiting period.

You can do part or all of the construction work yourself or hire a contractor to build your project.

An alternative to hiring a contractor, particularly when you plan to do most of the work yourself, is to hire helpers. Good sources of helpers are the services ads in your newspaper, or the nearest high school, college, or technical school, which may have a job placement program for students. Neighborhood youngsters looking for part-time work also make good helpers for landscaping projects.

Permits

Whether you will need a building permit depends on the scope of your plan. If your plans call for landscape work only, such as putting in plants, shrubs, trees, walls less than 3 feet high, or sprinkler systems, you probably will not need a permit. You also do not normally need a building permit to install or construct a garden tool shed that occupies 120 square feet or less of floor space. But if you are putting in outdoor lighting, decks, patios, driveways—anything that involves structural work or electrical changes—you will need a permit. If you are in doubt, just call the building inspector's office, usually found in city hall.

While many people grumble about the costs and bureaucracy involved in obtaining them, permits do serve a purpose in maintaining health and safety standards in a community. If someone installed a swimming pool on the slope above your house, wouldn't you sleep better knowing he had to meet specific codes so all that water wouldn't one day spill from the pool into your backyard? At the same time, the inspector's office can offer useful advice on your plans, to make sure you do everything "to code."

To obtain a permit, you will have to submit plans (usually two sets) to the inspector's office. They will be checked and either approved or sent back for required code changes. Once plans are approved, you may start work. An inspector will then visit the site at certain stages of the work to see that it is done properly. You must call the building inspector's office a few days ahead of time to request a visit, so plan your work to prevent unnecessary delays.

Two common ordinances to keep in mind when drawing up plans are local zoning ordinances and setback requirements. In some areas, zoning laws limit the percentage of the lot that can be covered with buildings or paving. In addition, often there are setback requirements specifying that any construction must be kept a certain distance from the property lines. Be sure to check these two requirements in your area.

If your plans conflict with local ordinances but you feel you are in the right, you can request a variance. This is an exception to the rule that may be granted by the local appeal board or city council after they hear your argument. Variances provide some flexibility to the rigid requirements usually laid down by local governments. One of the chief considerations for approving a variance request is evidence that you will not impose on your neighbor's rights. You may want to have your neighbor appear with you at the variance hearing to make your case stronger.

For major landscaping projects, consider renting power equipment to make the work easier and quicker.

Estimating Costs and Materials

Estimating costs and materials is largely a matter of counting up everything needed and checking its price. The trick is not to overlook anything. Estimates should be done while the plan is in the concept stage so you can add or subtract projects, depending on your budget.

To make an accurate cost estimate, you must first have a good estimate of the materials you are going to need. Using your plans, break down your materials requirements into as many categories as necessary. For example, you may need one section to cover all the plant material, another for the watering system, and a detailed lumber list for projects such as a deck or a gazebo.

Once this list is complete, visit a nearby nursery, retail lumber dealer, and hardware store to get a general idea of the cost of most items on your list. For instance, you might want to find out the cost per lineal foot for decking lumber. (It is often sold in board feet, equivalent to a 12-inch length of 1 by 12, but the lumber counter can quickly convert it for you; at any rate, a lineal foot and a board foot of 2 by 6, the most common deck lumber, is the same). In estimating costs, it will pay to visit several different suppliers since costs can vary considerably; also keep an eye out for sales. And if you are buying in a large quantity, do not hesitate to ask for a discount.

More detailed information on calculating material needs is given in the sections on wood, brick, stone, and concrete.

Scheduling

Once your plans are ready, it's tempting to start construction. This is when you must stay patient. Starting a job without an overall plan of attack is a sure way to become mired down in the middle of it.

Materials Cost Estimate (partial)

Phase One: Site Preparation

Drop box rental: three days use of 20 cubic yard box	$ 67.
Herbicide cost: for weed control	25.
Soil amendment: nitrified sawdust. 2″ depth x 3500 square feet = 21 cubic yards at $18.50 delivered (plus tax)	400.
Tiller rental: 1 day at $65. per day	65.
Tractor rental: ½ day at $50. per half day	50.
Phase One Subtotal	**$607.**

Phase Two: Drainage

Trencher rental: 5 hours at $15. per hour	$ 75.
Drain rock: 350 linear feet trench, at 1 cubic foot rock per 2 linear feet trench = 170 cubic feet = 6.5 cubic yards plus 15 cubic feet for 2 French drains = total of 7 cubic yards at $20. per yard delivered (plus tax)	155.
Drain line: 280′ of 3″ perforated flex drain plus 100′ of 3″ solid flex drain = total of 380′ at 35 cents per foot	133.
Drain line fittings: 4-downspout connectors at $.60 8-couplings at $.65 6-"Y" connectors at $1.60 3-tee connectors at $1.20 7-end caps at $.80 (plus tax)	28.
Phase Two Subtotal	**$391.**

Phase Three: Construction

Concrete walks: forms—300′ 1x4 at $.25=$75. 200′ bender board at $.16 = $32. concrete—150′ path length = 3.5′ width = 4″ depth = 175 cubic feet finished concrete. This equals 7 cubic yards bulk ready mix at $60. per yard delivered (plus tax) = $420. reinforcing mesh—525 square feet at $.30 per square foot plus tax = $170.	
Total for concrete paths	$697.
Expose aggregate concrete patio: forms—400′-2x4″ rough redwood forms (permanent headers) at $.60 per foot	240.
Phase Three Subtotal	**$937.**

Plant List

Trees

Number	Size	Botanical Name	Common Name	Notes
1	15 gal	Prunus yedoensis 'Akedbono'	Flowering cherry	
1	15 gal	Abies concolor	White fir	When large enough, prune so that the lowest branch is 7′ from the ground

Shrubs

Number	Size	Botanical Name	Common Name	Notes
9	5 gal	Contoneaster lacteus	Parney cotoneaster	Prune to an informal hedge
1	5 gal	Pinus mugo 'mugo'	Mugo pine	
	5 gal	Camelia japonica 'Magnoliaeflora'	Camellia	
13	1 gal	Punus caroliniana	Carolina laurel cherry	Prune to an informal hedge

Note: Costs shown not necessarily current. Check local suppliers for current costs.

Often the do-it-yourselfer realizes, halfway through a job, that it can't be finished until another job is done, and that other job can't be finished until a smaller project is completed. The resulting confusion has led to many an uncompleted project.

Before beginning the actual work, prepare a job schedule. This schedule will spell out the most efficient job sequence for the whole project. It's easy enough to say, "Well, I know what needs to be done," and if you are highly organized, that's fine. For most of us, though, job schedules are essential and provide motivation.

To draw up the work schedule, first look over your plans and list all the jobs to be done, without regard to priority. These might include putting in shrubbery, laying water lines, constructing patios, building decks, or installing underground lighting.

Now take a piece of paper and draw a horizontal line to represent the progress of the project from beginning to end. Give some thought to the matter and then chart the jobs in the most logical and smoothest sequence. Generally, any job requiring large equipment is done first because heavy machinery may damage smaller projects. Plantings and other finishing touches are reserved for last.

Your scheduling should allow time for every part of the job, even those that are often overlooked, such as hiring extra help on the larger projects, renting equipment when needed, and shopping around to select the material you need. Ordering material, you will find, can be quite time-consuming. It is also not uncommon to find that the particular item you want is not in stock and will take two weeks to get. That delay must be worked into your schedule.

When making up your schedule, remember to add the time needed for any remodeling or reconstruction. Breaking up and hauling away an old sidewalk can take a lot of time. Keep in mind seasonal weather patterns, too, so that you are not trying to build a deck when the mud is knee-deep in your backyard.

You and your friends can have fun and get a lot accomplished during one weekend working on a construction project like this attached deck.

GARDEN PROJECTS

If you have been wondering what to do with that bleak space called a yard, you are about to be handed a catalog of ideas. Just take your pick of projects as you thumb through the following pages filled with photographs and illustrations that are bound to spur your imagination. Even if you have a well-established yard, you will find designs here to give your property that added special touch.

As you will see, there are ideas here to tie together and enhance all the areas of the yard. The success of a landscaping project depends largely upon whether all the elements of the yard have been integrated into a cohesive pattern. For instance, your house can be linked to the yard by a patio or deck, while the deck may be connected by a pathway to a flower garden at the other end of the yard; the pathway, in turn, can be tied to the rest of the property by a nearby stone wall.

One of the most important reasons for landscaping is to create outdoor living spaces. A deck is an outdoor living space, but so is a simple garden bench under a shade tree. Your creations need not be complex; indeed, those that imitate the simple beauty of nature are often the most effective.

One last suggestion before you start: consider how your plans may affect your neighbors. A little imagination and advance planning will help prevent conflicts. A fence that may be attractive on your side may not fit in with your neighbor's lawn at all. In such a case, you'll need to work out something that is mutually acceptable. Who knows? You may even end up splitting the cost and the labor of a "good neighbor" fence.

The design of this carefully thought-out garden reflects its owner's tastes and provides a serene and secluded retreat.

Patios and terraces should be considered outdoor living areas, not just places to put a lawn chair or barbecue. People and furniture are as much a consideration outside the house as they are inside.

The main difference between indoor space and outdoor space is that the size of an outdoor room is flexible. Areas can be large or small, depending on your scale of entertaining and the available square footage. A patio can be one of the least expensive ways to add more living space to your home.

Besides patios, outdoor living areas can include entry courts, swimming pool decks, atriums, game courts, playgrounds, and garden work centers. There need be no conflict between beauty and practicality. A single brick may not be particularly beautiful, but look how beautiful and practical a brick patio is.

The location, size, shape, and choice of materials for a patio are best determined by its intended uses and the appropriateness of the design to the site. Of course, you will also want to consider your personal preferences and the cost.

The design of your patio will also be affected by how much activity will occur there, and how much openness or privacy is desired. Keep in mind, too, that while a patio can enhance any yard, paving a large portion of your grounds—particularly with concrete—may result in a commercial look. This can be avoided by visually breaking up the patio into smaller units with a variety of floorings, such as brick and wood, or flagstone and concrete. Large patio areas can also be divided by positioning plants, benches, or shade structures to screen areas with different uses.

Top: *A patio becomes a favorite place for summertime activities.*
Bottom: *Brick squares divide this patio into smaller, more appealing units.*

A patio can serve as an
outdoor kitchen or garden
work center.

Patio Types

Patios evolved from Persian traditions, and the concept was brought to the United States by Spanish settlers from Mexico who made their homes in New Mexico and California. In these warm climates, courtyards provided an overflow space for living, just as today's patio does. Because interior rooms often opened directly onto it, the courtyard was the center of the household activity. In the courtyards were wells, flowers, herbs, and trees, as well as pleasant places to sit in the shade.

Often, a patio is a smooth extension of the house, allowing you to step from the living room inside to the living room outside. But a patio can also be positioned under a shade tree in the yard, or in a small nook in the garden where you can read while watering the tomatoes.

There are as many types of patios as there are rooms in a house. Some are functional, serving as an outdoor kitchen, complete with barbecue, sink, and cold running water. Others are geared toward social activities, and mimic the intimacy of a living room, complete with comfortable furniture. Still others are like a study, providing a quiet, plant-filled retreat from the bustle of the house. They can be simple and natural or elaborately equipped with fire pits and outdoor lighting for the evenings.

This courtyard matches the
Spanish style typical of the
desert Southwest.

Outdoor rooms can be furnished in the summer for sleeping outdoors on mats, hammocks, or Japanese *futons*. Where indoor space is limited, structures on the patio may house laundry equipment, storage cupboards, and garbage cans.

Patios serve many uses other than providing a space for sitting outdoors. Often, they become sport centers, used for games ranging from table tennis to shuffleboard. Patios are also popular sites for hot tubs and spas. These can be built off the master bedroom for privacy, or off the living room for family enjoyment.

It would be nice to say that changing an ordinary backyard into a delightful patio garden is a fairly easy task. Actually, it requires work—and sometimes lots of it, depending on the complexity of your design and the degree of difficulty involved in putting a new surface on a part of your grounds. But, in the end, it is worth all the effort. A well-designed patio can add considerably to the value of your property, and will add to your enjoyment of the yard.

Design and Construction Considerations

When you start planning your patio, one of your first considerations will be determining the access to the patio from the house. Does the living room open directly onto space you could use for a patio, or will you have to go through the kitchen to reach it?

Until recently, many architects didn't consider access to the garden area important, and left only a narrow back door to reach the garden. If the structure of your house does not provide direct and easy access, you may want to modify the area of the house nearest to the garden to provide a comfortable flow between the inside and outside entertaining areas. Often, a doorway can replace a window, or a sliding glass door can be installed in a solid wall.

Top: *Contrasting boulders and bricks make this hot tub an attractive focal point.*

Bottom: *For pool areas, select bricks that won't be slippery when wet.*

20

It is worth your while to spend several hours walking about your grounds to find just the right location for your patio, whether it will be attached to the house or some distance away. As you study the potential sites, imagine the views in all directions. Visualize, too, how the patio will look from inside the house, or from the street.

This initial study of the land should be done before you start designing the patio, because the better you know the land, the better you will see its design potential.

The actual design of your patio will probably be a distillation of the many design ideas you have collected. From the pictures here and in magazines you will start to see what design best suits your tastes. The size of your lot will also be a factor. On a small lot, the patio may be enclosed and cozy; on a country estate, it may be spacious and free-flowing. As creative ideas occur while you are reading, jot down your thoughts, or circle details that you want to use.

In your design plans, be sure to incorporate the facilities you want, such as a barbecue, planters, or storage areas. Consider using different pavings to designate special areas, or installing raised planters to better define the space. The advance planning you do will be one of the most enjoyable parts of the patio construction, so take your time to develop the best ideas. In planning your patio, you will want to consider several items:

■ Paving materials will be a leading consideration, because they will help set the tone of the whole area. They may be brick laid on sand, irregular patterns of textured concrete, or blocks of redwood or pressure treated pine laid like bricks.

■ The surface you choose will be determined, in part, by what activities you plan there. A family with young, active children may want a combination of grass and concrete to provide year-round play areas. Others may want small nooks with wooden floorings where they can relax in peace and quiet.

■ Another consideration is ease of maintenance. How much time do you have to work in and around the patio, and how much work do you want to do? A patterned concrete patio, while difficult to install, is virtually maintenance-free. Bricks on sand require occasional repair as bricks crack or sink out of line in the sand.

■ Apart from regular maintenance, there is the question of just how much work you want to do in order to improve your property. Your patio should harmonize with the existing terrain, but if your yard is sloped steeply, that could mean building a series of terraces. You will need to decide whether to do the work yourself, hire a contractor to do it, or choose another type of outdoor living area, such as a deck.

Asphalt makes an attractive paving (top), but concrete paving (bottom) is easier for the do-it-yourselfer.

■ The cost of your patio is a final consideration, but don't let it deter you from having what you want. Even if you must add to the patio every month or so, as money and time become available, you should build the kind of patio you like. Installing a lower quality patio just to save money will leave you with an outdoor living space you don't enjoy, and therefore won't use much.

Materials

All too often, a patio consists of a simple 10-foot-square slab of concrete just outside the back door. Though functional, this design fails to take advantage of the many materials available for patio construction. If you already have this sort of patio, you don't have to rip it out, just consider it the first step in a patio expansion program. Often, it makes an ideal spot for a covered area that can be used when it is too sunny or wet to use the rest of the patio.

Whether you are planning a new patio from bare ground or expanding an existing one, a balanced use of different materials can make your patio sparkle. This does not mean you should use all the different materials at once, or in equal amounts, which would result in a confusing patchwork of patterns. But the subtle use of a contrasting material, such as railroad ties laid next to aggregate, or red brick edging along concrete, gives the effect of trimwork. It brings definition to the patio.

Although many materials can be used in patio construction, the most popular materials are concrete, brick, and flagstone. These can be used by themselves or in combination with each other.

Concrete. Of these three materials, concrete is the cheapest and easiest to use, but also the most plain by itself. Still, there are many ways to disguise concrete. Concrete can be divided into sections by using redwood or treated wood crosspieces to break up the broad expanse.

Bender board forms can be used to make the outline of the concrete curve fit any pattern. And the concrete surface need not be just a gray slab, either. It can be colored, stamped with special tools to resemble brick or cobblestones, imprinted with designs, or "seeded" on top with bright stones.

If a concrete patio still seems drab to you, you might want to enhance it with borders of brick, or add brick or wood planters set on the concrete at strategic locations. Another way to use concrete is to make your own paving blocks by pouring concrete into forms of the size and shape you want. The blocks are then set directly into the lawn to form the patio. Techniques for working with concrete are discussed in more detail beginning on page 88.

Brick. Brick remains one of the most popular materials for a patio because of its warm appearance, its compatibility with almost any house and landscape style, and its relatively easy installation.

Brick patios are generally constructed in one of two ways: either laid on sand, which requires a rigid perimeter form, or mortared onto a slab. If you already have a concrete slab patio or a concrete sidewalk, you can revitalize it by mortaring bricks over it. Instead of using full-size bricks, you can buy bricks that are just ½ inch thick and are put in place on a bed of epoxy glue.

Bricks are available in a variety of textures; your choice will depend upon how you intend to use your patio area. A smoothly finished brick may be perfect for the barbecue area but, because it will be slippery when wet and may reflect too much glare in the summer, it may not be suited for use around a pool. Used bricks, on the other hand, are sometimes considered too rough to provide a comfortable walking or playing surface. More details on different types of brick and their uses is found beginning on page 80.

This outdoor living area incorporates several different types of building materials without looking either cluttered or haphazard.

Brick-on-Sand Patio

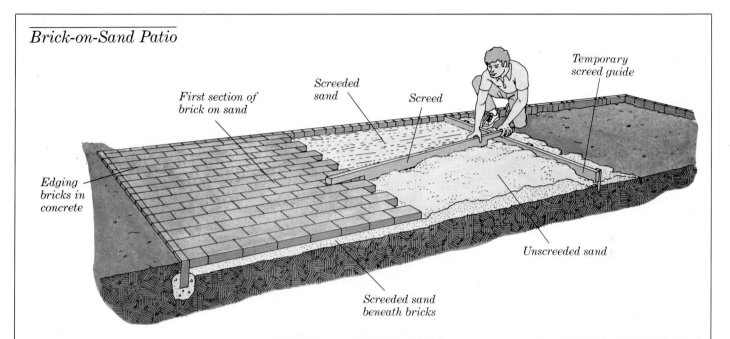

First section of brick on sand

Screeded sand

Screed

Temporary screed guide

Edging bricks in concrete

Unscreeded sand

Screeded sand beneath bricks

Flagstone. Flagstone makes a particularly elegant patio. For an enduring one, it should be mortared in place on a concrete slab. Individual flagstones can also be set directly in the lawn, nicely complimenting the textures of rock and grass. Flagstone can be set in a bed of sand, but this method is not recommended because the stones will not fit tightly together and the sand between the pieces can easily be swept out, dislodging the stones. See page 86 for more information on stonework.

Finishing Details

Just as beautiful trim work inside the house sets off a room, attention to details in your outside room can make the difference between an ordinary and an extraordinary patio. Some of these features include edging, especially edging made of contrasting materials, and tree wells.

Edgings. In most cases, the limits of your patio should be sharply defined. A distinctive border can create a strong sense of perimeter, marking where the concrete patio ends and the grass begins. It might seem that grass and concrete alone would provide a striking enough contrast, but an edging of brick, stone, or wood provides needed definition.

A flagstone patio is natural in appearance and so inherently beautiful that it complements almost any type of landscape.

23

Bricks are one of the most popular edging materials. With brick, you'll find that the placement technique greatly affects the final appearance of the edging. The most efficient method for covering a large surface is to place the bricks end to end with the broad face up. But compare that effect to the appearance of bricks placed side by side with the longer sides together and the broad face up. Next, compare that to bricks placed face to face with the narrow edge up. Each step in this progression is a step up in detail, and detail is what makes a perimeter striking. Bricks also can be set with the ends angled up or cemented in place on top of a poured concrete edging.

If you want bold edging, consider using heavy timbers. Railroad ties are an excellent border material, but are sometimes difficult to find. Alternatives include sections of old telephone poles or pressure treated timbers. Where timbers are butted together as edgings, cut the corners at a 45-degree angle for a more finished appearance.

Edging

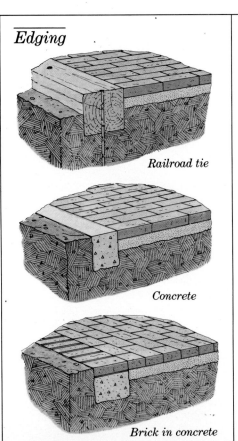

Railroad tie

Concrete

Brick in concrete

Bricks on edge

Board

Edging adds needed definition to a patio. Choose a material or color that contrasts with the patio material, like these red bricks bordering a concrete aggregate patio.

For curved effects with wood borders, you can make a partial saw cut, or kerf, through 2 by 4s or 2 by 6s along the inside edge to make them more flexible. Cut no more than halfway through the board, with cuts spaced about 2 inches apart for gentle curves and about ½ inch apart for tight curves.

Easier to shape are redwood bender boards that can be nailed together for greater strength after they are in place. Supporting stakes can be covered with soil.

Tree Wells. If you are planning on raising the level of your patio area with dirt, but there is a lovely tree on the site, you will not be able to build the dirt up around the tree without killing it. The solution is to build a tree well.

One way to do this is to build up the fill to the level you want and then sculpt it back in a sweeping cup around the tree. The bottom should be level with the original grade. The space between the fill and the tree can then be filled with large rocks, which brings the area around the tree up to the new grade but still allows the trunk of the tree to breathe. If you use this method, you will have to check with a certified nursery to see whether your particular tree can take the weight of the rocks.

For a more elaborate well, the cup could be lined with bricks on sand, a mixture that is porous enough to let water drain through.

For deeper wells, construct a redwood or treated-wood box around the tree—something like a planter box set in the ground. Be sure to leave lots of room for the tree to move in the wind and for its trunk to grow. Use heartwood, redwood, or wood pressure-treated with waterborne preservatives for the best resistance to decay. Top it with a 2 by 6 cap to make a comfortable garden seat.

Be careful to construct a tree well with ample drainage so the roots will not stand in a pool of water all winter and drown.

Tree wells need not detract from a landscape. Here they become a striking focal point, accented by the circular pattern of stone paving.

Decks are one of the easiest and fastest means of creating outdoor living spaces. Unlike patios that must be placed on fairly level ground, decks can be built anywhere—over level ground or steep slopes, or even over rocky ledges.

A beautiful deck beside a house, even if built almost flush with the ground, makes an effective transition from the yard to the house and provides a relaxing entertainment area.

With a little patience, decks can be built by anyone who knows the basics of using a hammer and saw.

A deck should be built with attention to the primary uses it will serve. It may be a direct extension of the house, the flooring for a tree-shaded hideaway, or a child's play area. Like people, decks have their own distinct characteristics.

There are decks for privacy and seclusion, decks open to the world and the sun, multilevel decks for free-wheeling parties, decks that can accommodate half the kids in the neighborhood, and decks for quiet dining.

Decks can also be divided into sections, or placed at different levels, to give you different living spaces within the same area.

Deck construction can range from the very simple to the complex, depending on the terrain around your house and how ambitious your plans are. While you can certainly build your own deck, some of you may decide that much of the work is beyond your scope, particularly if the deck is to be built on a steep slope. In this case, you can hire a professional to do the most difficult work, such as constructing the framework.

Before you start any deck construction, no matter how simple, plan it carefully and see that it is integrated into your overall yard plan.

Most decks will require a building permit, which means drawing up plans, having them copied, and submitting them to the local building inspector's office.

Deck Types

Deck types can be divided into two general categories: attached or free-standing. Yet, there are so many variations available that no two decks seem alike. The only limit is your imagination.

Decks are an ideal way to create usable outdoor space on flat terrain (top) or on steep slopes (bottom).

The attached deck is fixed to an existing building, generally to the side of the house, but it could be built off a garden shed, tool house, or any other structure. Because one side is anchored to an existing building, the attached deck is generally easier to build than the freestanding deck.

Building a freestanding deck can be simple or complicated, depending on the type of terrain you must deal with. If you have a level yard and would like a lounging deck in one part of it, you can simply place three railroad ties or treated 4 by 4 beams on the ground, space them 4 feet apart and level them, then nail 2 by 6 redwood or pressure-treated boards to them, and you will have a free-standing deck.

Generally, however, decks require the installation of footings and piers, plus posts and beams, as part of the supporting structure. This allows you to put a deck over irregular or sloping ground. For details on deck construction, see Ortho's book *How To Design and Build Decks and Patios.*

Decks can be created in an infinite variety of styles. They can be built all on one plane or on two or more levels to create separate seating and entertaining areas. A multitiered deck is ideal when you want to build over steeply sloping ground. Instead of jutting a deck out into the air, high off the ground, let it descend in a series of pods, linked by stairways.

In rocky areas, interesting decks can be built right among the rocks, twisting and turning like a flowing wooden stream following the rock pattern. Here, careful cutting is required to make the decking fit around the rocks. The result of such careful work is that the rocks seem to be an integral part of the deck.

If you have a tree right where you want the deck, don't cut down the tree. Build the deck around it. The tree will offer both beauty and shade. You cannot anchor the deck to the tree, however, since tree movement due to wind would destroy the deck. Instead, you build the deck around it, leaving enough room for the tree to

grow and to move on windy days.

Decks can also be constructed on top of flat-roofed garages, or over extensions to the main house. In these cases, the original structure must have been built to withstand the additional load of a deck. This means the rafters have to be large enough,

depending on the length of their span, to handle the weight of the decking plus the weight of guests, tables, chairs, and other furniture. If you are thinking of constructing such a deck, consult a licensed contractor or an architect first.

These decks invite active use by using outdoor lighting (top) and incorporating the spectacular view (bottom).

Design and Construction Considerations

In designing a deck, take particular note of the lay of the land, then design the deck to complement the terrain. The deck may curve along a retaining wall or it may step down in a series of platforms that follow a stream or ravine. The deck need not be a simple square, but may contain angles or curves to shape it to the surrounding grounds.

The site you choose for the deck should be directly related to its primary uses. For entertaining near the house, it will probably be most convenient to locate it next to the dining room, living room, or family room.

But you can also add your own special decks, off a bedroom or around a favorite shade tree in the yard, for instance. In picking a site, consider such factors as whether there is good drainage under the deck, particularly if it is close to the ground, and whether it will be too hot in direct sun. Problems with the sun can be corrected, however, as you will see in the section on shade structures on pages 56-61.

When you design the deck itself, keep in mind the essential elements of deck construction. These include the footings, piers, posts, beams, joists, and decking. For solid decking, use 2 by 4 or wider lumber over joists spaced 16 inches apart, measured from center to center.

Decking Patterns

The size and shape of the deck and the plank size and pattern of the decking determine the framing plan of the deck.

In diagonal patterns, the decking may be laid at any angle greater than 45 degrees or less than 90 degrees to the joists. Standard framing may be used for diagonal decking as long as you note that the span between joists must be measured at the same angle as the decking. Also, the joists must be set closer together than for standard decking.

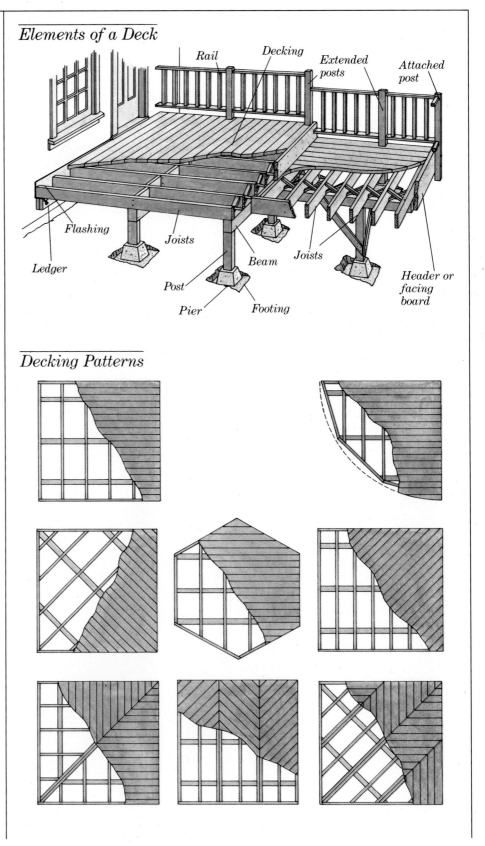

Elements of a Deck

Rail · Decking · Extended posts · Attached post · Flashing · Ledger · Joists · Post · Pier · Footing · Beam · Joists · Header or facing board

Decking Patterns

Decking on Edge. An attractive deck can be made by placing 2 by 4s on edge. This requires considerably more time and effort, not to mention more wood, but the result is a deck that is unusually strong and attractive. Wood spacers are required near the ends and over each joist.

Parquet Decks. These are generally laid out in 3- or 4-foot grids, so the size of the deck should be in multiples of 3 or 4. If this is not possible, you can still have a parquet deck by designing it in 3- or 4-foot grids and then finishing the outer edges with a contrasting design that will appear as a border trim. Since most lumber comes in even lengths, a 4-foot grid will have less waste than a 3-foot grid.

Parquet decks are often laid directly on the ground. The area should be excavated first to allow for 2 inches of pea gravel for drainage and room for the depth of the deck so the finished deck is level with the surface of the yard.

Deck Materials
Many different materials go into the construction of a deck, but the deck-builder's first consideration is usually what type of wood will be used.

Decks are commonly built with redwood, cedar, or cypress, all of which are naturally rot resistant if made from heartwood. In addition, decks are increasingly being built with pressure-treated lumber that resists rot. If you use pressure-treated lumber, make sure the treatment is a waterborne preservative, which is clean, odorless, and can either be stained or painted.

Your choice of lumber will depend, in part, on what is available where you live and what you can afford to pay. On the West Coast, for example, redwood is commonly used for decks, but it is prohibitively expensive on the East Coast.

Unless you have a very simple deck that simply lies on flat ground, you will need all of the following in addition to the decking material: 4 by 4 or larger timber, concrete piers with concrete footings to support them, posts, beams, joists, and (if the deck is attached to the house), a ledger board bolted to the house.

If you have a ledger board on the house, you will need flashing (strips of sheet metal) over it so rainwater won't work its way behind the siding and cause rot. You will also need joist hangers to support the joists; the hangers are purchased to match the size of joists you are using.

Nails are, of course, essential, since almost all the deck framing is attached with 16d nails. To nail down the decking, use stainless steel or hot-dipped galvanized (not electroplated galvanized) nails. Stainless steel nails cost more, but they won't leave you with the stains that appear about a year after a deck is laid with less costly nails.

For more details on the types of wood and other materials used in deck construction, see pages 74-79.

Finishing Details
A neatly finished platform, a handsome railing, and attractive benches are some of the elements that can set your deck apart from others. Careful attention to the finishing touches is just as important as building a solid base and laying an even decking surface in the final appearance of your deck.

Railings. There is almost no limit to the variety of attractive railing designs, but there are a few basic rules. Some building codes require railings, especially when the decks are 3 feet or higher above the ground.

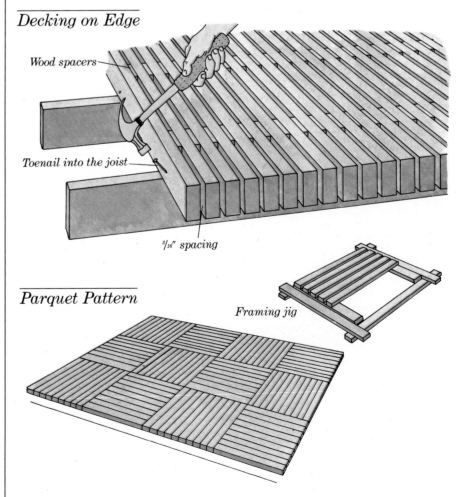

Decking on Edge

Wood spacers

Toenail into the joist

³/₁₆" spacing

Parquet Pattern

Framing jig

First, railings must be strong enough to support people leaning on or sitting on them. If the deck is more than 3 feet off the ground, or if small children will ever be on the deck, the railing should be designed to prevent anyone falling over or through the rails. Your local code will usually specify the maximum opening.

Deck railings are constructed either on posts that extend through the deck from the substructure, or on posts fastened to the deck. The first method is stronger but somewhat more complicated to construct.

A very secure post can also be made by clasping a joist on each side with two 2 by 4 or 2 by 6 uprights to form the post. This method works well where benches are to be built into the deck as part of the railing.

A cap board, although not used on many railings, does add a finished look and provides a handy rest to lean on or to place drinks on. The cap should be wider than the posts; with 4 by 4 posts you would normally use a 2 by 6 cap, leaving an equal overhang on each side of the post.

Note the details that make this railing special: the angled ends of the rails and the grooved, slanted post tops.

Railing Construction

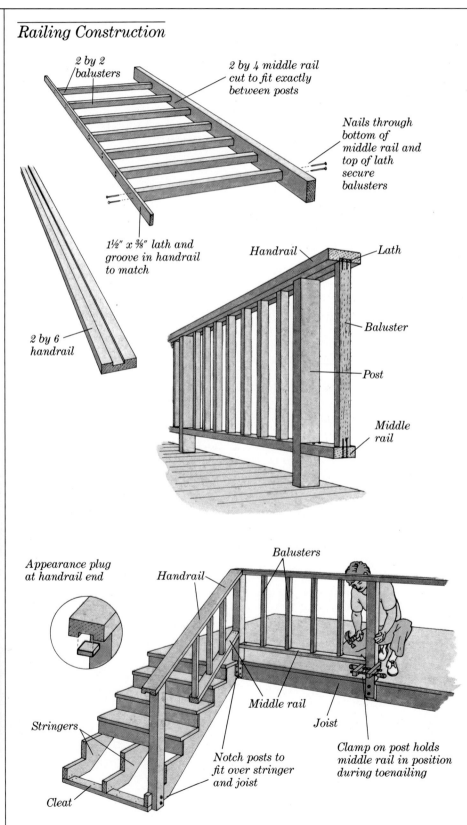

Once the cap is in place, you can add an even more finished look to the deck, and minimize the chance of splinters by using a router to round the edges along the cap.

The design of your railing can follow any of the styles shown here or it can follow a pattern you create yourself. The more complex your railing design, the longer it will take to complete, but in the long run the extra effort will prove worthwhile. The railing is one of the most visible aspects of a deck, and since you are going to be looking at it for years to come, you will want to take the time to create a distinctive design.

Benches. If your deck is just a foot or so off the ground, it may not need a railing. You can add a finishing touch to such a low-profile deck by installing benches around the edges. These not only provide a visual limit to the deck—so guests won't have the sense that they could inadvertently fall off the edge—but they provide a convenient place to sit and relax, eliminating the need for furniture.

Benches can be either built-in or freestanding. They may have backs that form a railing or, if the deck is close to the ground, they may be low, wide platforms that serve as both railings and seating areas.

Particularly attractive benches can be made from 2 by 4s laid on edge and separated by wood spacers about 1 inch thick. The wood can be curved by cutting a series of kerfs on the inside of the curve, then forcing the boards into the desired curve. Make the cuts one-third the thickness of the 2 by 4 and space them about 1 inch or less apart.

Benches are easily constructed around railing posts. Simply bolt two 2 by 4s to each post about 14 inches above the deck and extend them out 15 to 18 inches. A 4 by 4 clasped at the end forms the outer leg of the bench. Form the bench on these supports by adding 2 by 4s spaced far enough apart to allow rain to run off. Finally, face the ends of the 2 by 4s with lengths of 1 by 6 for a more finished look.

Benches are as variable as decks. Possible designs include freestanding (top), with back that forms a railing (middle), or curved (bottom).

WALKS AND PATHS

Walks and paths are the links in the chain of elements that make up your yard, and they are one of the most flexible elements you can use in the design of your garden.

Your idea of a pathway shouldn't be limited to that narrow strip of concrete we call a sidewalk. Paths can be constructed of brick, aggregate, concrete, wood, or any combination of these materials. They can also take any form imaginable, following a curving hedge, skirting a deck, circling a reflecting pool, or inviting a stroll around your flower beds.

Design and Construction Considerations

There is more to planning walks and paths than you might imagine. In addition to figuring out the number of paths you will need and their general direction, you will have to determine how wide they must be, the materials you will use, and how the paths will be incorporated into your overall yard plan.

Walkways are quite easy to build. Even an inexperienced carpenter or mason will be able to build most of the examples shown in these pages.

One of the most important walkways is the one that leads to the front door of the house. Like the surrounding yard and the front of the house, the walkway plays a key part in setting the tone for the entire yard.

In most cases you will already have a front walk, though you may want to expand or redesign it. Since the square footage involved in a front walk is usually relatively small, you may be able to use more expensive paving materials here. Brick, flagstone, or exposed aggregate concrete, are all excellent choices.

A walk does not have to be straight and plain. Curves make a walkway interesting and more inviting.

Many walkways are too narrow. Entry paths should be wide enough for two people to walk abreast. For entries, a walkway 4 to 5 feet wide is best, and if the walk is next to the house or a retaining wall, it can be made a little wider so people's shoulders won't brush against the wall. Garden walks can be narrower, down to 30 inches wide, but a path that is at least 36 inches wide is more comfortable.

You may want to vary the width of the walkway slightly to provide more visual interest. Gentle curves and subtle direction changes will get you from point A to point B in a fairly direct manner while avoiding the monotony of a straight concrete walk.

Even if you have that straight ribbon of concrete leading to the front of the house, you can still improve its appearance. One method is to lay a brick on sand border on each side of and level with the walk. This makes the walkway appear nearly twice as wide and provides a colorful border.

In many cases, the driveway also serves as an entrance walk. If you add a strip of paving material parallel to the driveway, guests will have room to maneuver around parked cars and the additional paving will provide a pleasant contrast to the driveway paving.

In laying out paths and walks, take a close look at your terrain. If there is a dip in the ground, will it be full of water in the winter or during a rain storm? If this is the case, put in a gravel-filled ditch first before you build the walk so the area will drain.

If your grounds are irregular, plan how you will get from one level to another. Steps are one solution, but you might also be able to build a path that follows the contours of the lot.

Try to imagine the traffic patterns that might develop in your yard. How do guests get from the curb to the front door? Will you have a convenient route from the car to the kitchen when your arms are full of grocery bags?

Materials

Much of the character of your walk will depend on the paving material you select. The choices are many depending on the desired color, texture, and style of walk. The most common paving materials are concrete, brick, flagstone, and wood.

Concrete. Concrete is the most common material used for walks, and by itself it is generally quite dowdy.

But concrete doesn't have to be plain. You can seed it with pretty stones, color it, stamp it with patterns, or cover it with brick or flagstone.

You can also make an interesting concrete walk out of concrete paving blocks. They are available in many shapes and sizes, many of them with interlocking edges for greater stability and design variation.

Stepping stones and concrete form walks with attractive but different styles in these two landscapes.

Brick. Brick and flagstone still set the tone for elegance in a walk because they blend so well with any decor. They are not only beautiful but highly durable.

There are many types of brick to choose from, at markedly different prices, sizes, and colors as a visit to your local masonry yard will reveal. The standard brick is approximately 7¾ by 3¾ by 2¼ inches, and weighs about 4 pounds. Similar in appearance is a ''brick'' made from concrete with coloring additives. Concrete bricks cost about one-third as much as clay bricks and are also an excellent choice for walks.

If you are aiming for a rustic or weathered look, you may want to build your walk with real used bricks, which are often quite expensive, or with simulated used bricks. The advantage in choosing used brick, real or not, is that your walkway immediately looks as if it has been in place for years. This can be important if you are installing a walk in a long-established garden.

Flagstone. Like brick, flagstone combines durability and elegance, and its natural rock surface highlights any garden. Although bricks can be placed tightly together on a bed of sand, flagstone cannot be laid on sand because of its irregular surfaces and edges. It must be mortared in place over a concrete walk or slab, or set directly in a lawn.

Many other materials can be used to make excellent walks at much less cost than brick or flagstone. Consider some of these:

Wood. For an informal effect, simply lay out plank stringers of 4 by 4 redwood or pressure-treated wood posts on the ground. Space them 3 feet apart and level them, then nail on 2 by 6s. For best results, the 4 by 4s should be placed on a 2-inch bed of sand or pea gravel so they will seat and steady themselves. This will also provide drainage underneath. To keep grass and weeds from growing through the boards, cover the ground underneath them with black polyethylene.

Walks can be as varied as people. Here 4 by 4 blocks of wood laid on end create a walk full of personality and charm. Pressure-treated wood or redwood heartwood are best choices.

Wood blocks fitted together make an inviting, rustic surface. Cut the blocks from 4 by 4 material, preferably of redwood, cedar, or cypress heartwood, or pressure-treated wood. Make each block 3 inches long and fit the blocks together on a 2-inch bed of sand. They must be held in place by a rigid border frame. When all the blocks are fitted tightly together, sweep dry sand back and forth over them until all the spaces between the blocks are filled, locking them in place.

Wood rounds make an even more informal setting and they are quite inexpensive, especially if you have timber you can cut yourself. While they are less permanent than wood planks or blocks or other materials, even if you use cedar or redwood, they are easily replaced. Bed the rounds in 2 inches of sand and fill the spaces with sand or bark chips.

Finishing Details

Like patios, walkways often need some edging, either to hold the material in place or to provide a bold outline. Permanent edging is always required for brick-on-sand walks.

Edging can range from a simple concrete outline to a bold design of your own. One common type of edging is a row of bricks laid on edge. To keep the bricks from working loose, they must be placed in a bed of mortar. Place the brick edging either in the upright position or angled. This method will provide a flush border for easy mowing.

Edging can be done with many other materials, some of which you may not even have to buy, such as river rock, stones from your yard, or old railroad ties.

For edging along curved walkways, you can use one or two layers of redwood heartwood or pressure-treated pine bender board that is staked in place. The stakes are nailed to the bender board and the tops of the stakes are then cut down below the top of the bender board so the edge of the board provides a smooth, curved outline.

Railroad ties or rough 4 by 4 lumber make a bold edging that provides a distinct contrast with the paving material of a walk or patio.

STAIRS AND STEPS

Whether you have stairs leading from a deck, patio steps between terraces, or walkway steps over irregular ground, they should be more than a means to get from one level to another.

The style of your steps should be clearly defined and dramatic. Their design should invite your guests to stroll through the garden, and they should lead the eye smoothly between the separate but related levels of the patio or garden.

Stairs and steps in a garden setting are divided into two basic types: steps for patios or walkways and stairs for decks. By definition, then, steps are built into the ground, while stairs are built above the ground.

Design and Construction Considerations

Safety is a key consideration in the design and construction of stairs and steps. The paving must be nonskid, particularly when wet. Railings should also be used wherever there is a need for additional stability, particularly for the benefit of the elderly and young children.

Stairs

Stairs, as opposed to garden steps set into embankments, require careful measuring and cutting. They are comprised of a riser (the vertical part), a tread where you step, and stringers to support the steps.

The stringers are normally 2 by 12s, which provide enough depth for the step notches to be cut out and still carry the weight. Stairs can also be placed between the stringers by using 2 by 4 cleats or angle irons.

Unless you make a conscious design decision to do otherwise, you should cut the treads for deck stairs from the same size lumber used for the decking.

The riser space can be left open or it can be closed. On high stairs, open risers may not be desirable because they leave open for view the often unfinished or unkempt area beneath the stairs and deck.

Stairs must have a constant ratio between riser and tread so there is no guesswork about where to place your foot. The exception is on the first step, which can have a shorter riser than the others, if this is necessary to make all the other risers even.

There are several ways of working out a comfortable riser-to-tread ratio. Household stairs commonly have a 7:11 ratio; that is, a 7-inch riser and an 11-inch tread. Stairs on decks, however, are often cut broader for a greater sense of stability. A 6:12 ratio is common. This type of stair is readily made by using two 2 by 6s as the tread and a 2 by 6 as the riser.

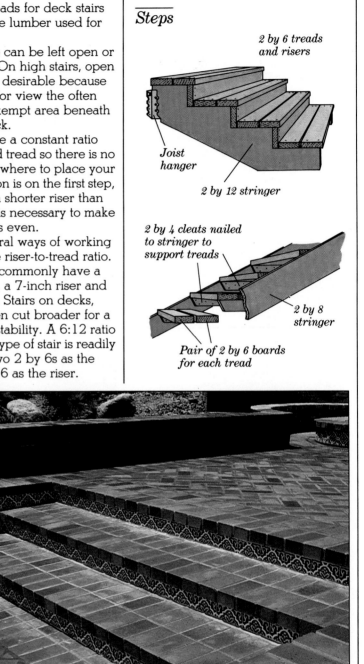

Steps

2 by 6 treads and risers

Joist hanger

2 by 12 stringer

2 by 4 cleats nailed to stringer to support treads

2 by 8 stringer

Pair of 2 by 6 boards for each tread

This patio features a herringbone pattern of bricks that contrasts with the straight pattern of the steps.

The front of the tread should overhang the riser by ½ inch to 1½ inches. This provides a shadow line that gives a look of depth to the stairs.

The top of the stringers should be securely fastened to the deck joists with 2 by 12 joist hangers. The bottom should rest on another deck, or on brick or concrete—never on bare ground where it will soon decay.

Steps

While steps should be attractive, they must also be comfortable and safe for walking. The tread area must be wide and stable underfoot, and the risers should not be so high that it is an effort to move up or down. As with stairs, the risers must be of equal height to prevent tripping, with the exception of the first riser which may be shorter than the others. In garden paths, where the steps may be far apart, they should be spaced evenly so people will not have to change stride each time they take a step.

Consider style, materials, and safety when designing stairs to connect different levels in your landscape or yard.

Riser-to-Tread Ratio

For proper ratio, add riser height to tread length. The sum should equal between 17 and 18 inches.

Stairs with risers higher than 8 inches and treads narrower than 9 inches are too steep for comfort.

Risers between 7 and 7⅝ inches and treads between 10 and 11 inches are the most comfortable.

Risers lower than 6 inches and treads wider than 11 are too flat, uncomfortable, and unsafe.

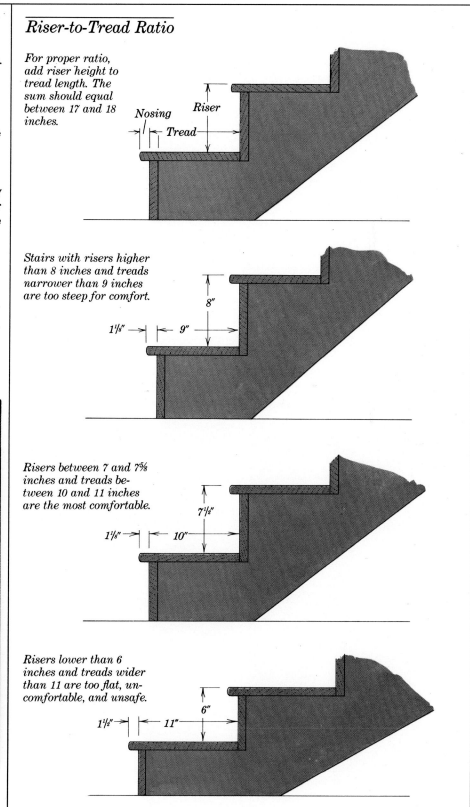

Another rule to follow is: the lower the riser, the wider the tread; this is both for the sake of comfort in walking and for appeal to the eye. Remember, too, that broad steps make inviting seating or planter areas.

The width of your steps will naturally depend on your own design and your site, but landscape designers generally feel that outdoor steps should be at least 4 feet wide for comfort and safety. In many cases, this may be too narrow. Stairs or steps that are 5 feet wide make it easy for a couple to walk side by side. Stairs 8 feet wide lend a sense of spaciousness to the entire patio or deck.

In planning the number of steps to descend an embankment, you must first calculate the angle of the slope.

Start by driving a stake where the top step will be. Directly in line with that stake, at the bottom of the slope, drive a stake that is tall enough to be at least level with the top of the slope.

Stretch a length of string or a straight 2 by 4 from the top stake directly over the bottom stake. Use a level to keep the string or board level. Measure the vertical distance from the bottom of the slope up to the string or board, and measure its horizontal length. This gives you the change in grade.

If, for instance, the vertical rise is 3 feet and the horizontal distance is 6 feet, the steps must rise 3 feet within the space of 6 feet. Draw these calculations on graph paper, using 6 inches for each square on the graph paper. Now work out the riser-to-tread ratio, which in this case is 3:6 or 6:12, which is acceptable for a deck.

If your particular embankment is so steep (for example, 4 feet of rise to 6 feet of horizontal distance for a ratio of 8:12) that you must have risers that are more than the height limit of 7 inches, consider the possibility of turning the steps so they zigzag or run up the slope at a lower angle.

Stairs are somewhat more complex to build than steps. If you have a steep area in your yard, consider putting in a stairway instead of cutting steps into the bank, which would require moving a lot of earth.

Railings

Railings often accompany steps and stairs, not just for safety but because they can be particularly attractive.

Building codes generally require railings only when stairs are connected to a building. In many cases, railings are not required when there are less than five risers.

But even if local codes do not call for railings, you will want to consider the number of children and elderly people who may use the steps. Add a railing if the distance between the top and bottom step is great enough that there is the slightest feeling of imbalance as you stand on the top step.

Steps of brick and heavy timbers are relatively easy to construct.

These concrete steps take on some personality with the added wood detail.

Local building codes may require sturdy railings where steps attach to buildings.

On many steps the railing may only be needed to provide a sense of reassurance, rather than a firm support. A chain or rope stretched between posts does well in these cases; guests will feel more comfortable just because it's there.

When there is a true railing, it is usually placed 30 to 34 inches above the treads. A simple wood railing consists of decay-resistant 4 by 4 posts bolted to the stair stringers or set 18 inches deep in concrete. Space the posts a maximum of 6 feet apart; a 4-foot interval is preferred. The posts can be capped with a 2 by 4, but using a 2 by 6 allows an attractive overhang on each side of the post. Edges should be rounded and sanded to prevent splinters.

For variation add decorative posts or a middle 2 by 4 rail. On decks, the stair railing should match the style of the deck railing.

Wrought-iron railings are another handsome and practical choice. They can be added to concrete or other masonry steps by drilling holes in the concrete and setting in the posts with a ready-mixed mortar. Brace the railings until the concrete cures.

Iron railings can also be attached to the sides of concrete steps with flanges. This is done by drilling holes in the concrete and fastening the flanges in place with lag screws.

Materials

Steps and stairways can be made from many different materials, as the photographs on these pages reveal. Often, the material is chosen to complement materials used elsewhere in the landscape. If you have a brick terrace, you may want to use brick to form the steps, or at least to put a border around concrete steps.

On the other hand, materials can also be chosen to provide a vivid contrast to the predominant texture in the garden. Rough railroad ties, for instance, provide an interesting contrast to a smooth patio of bricks.

Whether you use only a few materials to create a distinct contrast, or choose a larger number of closely related materials, the key word is balance for overall harmony.

The most common type of material for steps and stairs is wood. The wood for decks should match the deck material in species and in size. Garden steps can be made from many different types of wood but all should be decay-resistant, or you will find yourself replacing them every few years.

Concrete steps are practical, inexpensive, and long lasting. Once the form is built with 2 by 6s, all you need to do is pour the concrete. You can save a great deal of concrete by filling the center portion of each step with large rocks.

Concrete steps or stairs can later be covered with brick or mortar, trimmed with brick or wood, or finished with an exposed aggregate.

Place stepping stones equal distances apart for easy and safe walking.

FENCES

I**f you want to try your hand at a creative construction project, consider starting with a fence. Fences make perfect projects for beginning carpenters because they are not particularly difficult to build.**

The design possibilities are limitless. A fence can range from the purely utilitarian wire fence to a structure that is a work of art.

A fence gains beauty not only from its basic design, but from its setting and the care given to its construction. Witness a simple, rail fence snaking through the woods, curving with the terrain until it seems more a part of the land than a divider.

Before you begin to build a fence, give some thought to why you want or need one. No matter what the style, fences serve many purposes.

Privacy. While most communities restrict the height of fences in front yards, you may be able to enclose your back yard with a high fence. However, remember that even if privacy is your primary goal, your fence does not have to be solid and forbidding, or attractive on your side and an eyesore on the other. It can be a "good neighbor" fence of boards alternated on each side, or a lattice-work fence that suggests privacy while allowing in light and air.

Boundary Line. Fences that mark property lines are common in both suburban and rural settings. Here the fence is more a visual marker than an actual barrier. It simply defines the limits of the property, and defines the space within at the same time.

Security. Before you construct a fence designed to provide security—which means it will probably be at least 6 feet high—check your local building codes. Some communities have height restrictions for fences.

Top: *Even picket fences can have a unique flair.*
Bottom: *The wood lath adds style to a plain fence.*

*This 8-foot-tall fence utilizes
sheets of plywood.*

*This fence reveals the
builder's imagination.*

*This white lattice pattern
matches the garden style.*

*This jungle-style fence is
made from bamboo.*

*Pecky cypress improves a
simple board fence.*

*Wood shingles add a finished
look to this fence.*

*This "good neighbor" fence
has no bad side.*

*This tight woven fence has
verticals 12 inches apart.*

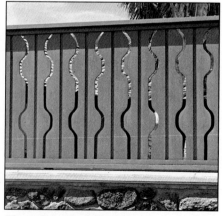

*These fence boards were
made with a band saw.*

If you do decide to build a fence for security purposes, remember that it doesn't have to be imposing to be effective. The harsh lines of a chain-link fence, for instance, can be softened with hedges or with slats of wood slipped through the links.

Buffer. In many areas, a high fence can protect against blustery winds. But unless the fence will be adjacent to the area needing protection, it should have many small openings rather than being solid. The openings break up the wind, which would swirl over the top of a solid fence. A fence can also provide protection from noise. A solid fence or a fence lined with thickly planted evergreens makes an excellent noise buffer.

The design of a fence should complement the entire style of the house and surrounding garden. A typical New England saltbox or Midwest Victorian invites a white picket fence, and, of course, a Kentucky horse ranch needs that white rail fence to complete the picture.

But you don't have to be restricted by these conventional patterns. A brick home, for instance, would look handsome with any of a number of different fence styles, from picket to stacked rails. Use the pictures on these pages as a source of inspiration for your own fence needs.

Design and Construction Considerations

Whatever its purpose, a fence generally makes a strong visual statement around your property.

If you want security, a 7-foot-high chain-link fence will make a very loud statement to that effect. But you can have a sense of security and definition of property with many other fence styles.

The fence may be in keeping with the surroundings, such as a stacked-rail fence winding through the trees, or it may be bold and sharply defined, such as a fence of canvas panels strung from a wooden frame.

Top: *An iron fence provides security without detracting from the view.*
Bottom: *A living fence creates an ever-changing landscape.*

A fence need not define the boundaries of the entire property. Instead, it may simply lead the eye to certain parts of the grounds, as a fence running out to encircle a garden does.

Whatever style of fence you choose, keep in mind that your house and property already have a style of their own, and the fence should be in keeping with that style.

Fencing should be an attractive addition to the yard or garden. Too often a fence is treated simply as a background for planting or a boundary marker rather than as a distinct part of the yard's design.

The type of terrain and special features of your yard will influence your choice of fence. Any style of fence can be put on level ground, but steep slopes call for careful planning. Some yards may have a section along a bluff or steep ravine that needs a child-proof fence.

Right: *The diagonal slats provide privacy but still let light and cool breezes through.*

Bottom: *This fence becomes part of the deck and shade structure.*

How to Build a Fence

1. Measure the entire area.

2. See how many posts you'll need.

3. Adjust the bays (openings between posts) near the end so all bays appear to be the same. Or split the width of the two end bays in half.

4. Mark corners with stakes and stretch twine between the stakes.

5. With a framing square, adjust corners as near to 90 degrees as possible. To make an exact right angle, measure 6 feet down one leg of twine from the corner, 8 feet down the other, and mark. Adjust twine until the diagonal measurement between the two marks is 10 feet.

6. Set all corner posts. With a posthole digger, and steel bar for hard ground, dig the posthole at least 18 inches deep; if possible, dig it 24 inches deep. Then stretch twine between them, if possible. If not, set intermediate posts to support twine over uneven ground. Make sure intermediate posts are in line with the end posts. Keep the twine about 2 feet off the ground.

7. Mark proper post spacing, then dig postholes. The base of the post must be in line with the twine, and the post must be plumb. Carefully check this with a level while the post is being set. Watch that a breeze does not blow the twine out of line.

8. Set the post on rocks or gravel to keep the base out of standing water.

9. Shovel about 6 inches of dirt around the base of the post. While a helper keeps the post plumb with the use of a level, and in line with string, tamp in the dirt.

10. Dirt must be dry to tamp properly. A post won't set in wet earth because it won't pack. In heavy clay mixture, add some pea gravel.

11. Add about 3 to 4 inches of dirt at a time to the hole, then tamp hard until the hole is full.

12. If posts later become slightly wobbly as the earth around them dries and shrinks, pour dry sand in the gap between the post and the surrounding dirt to retighten the post.

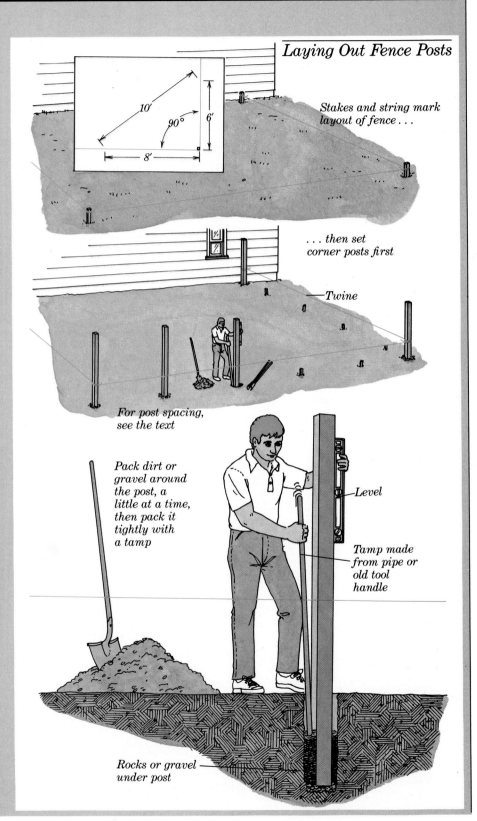

Laying Out Fence Posts

10'

90°

6'

8'

Stakes and string mark layout of fence . . .

. . . then set corner posts first

—*Twine*

For post spacing, see the text

Pack dirt or gravel around the post, a little at a time, then pack it tightly with a tamp

—*Level*

Tamp made from pipe or old tool handle

Rocks or gravel under post

You may also need a fence that children cannot climb around a swimming pool. Many local codes now require fences around pools.

Paying attention to site considerations also means considering your neighbors. Talk with them before you build, and try to come up with a design that both of you will be happy with. A compromise like this can sometimes lead to splitting the costs and the labor.

If the fence is to be placed on the property lines, check deed restrictions and verify your property lines before starting. It may even be a good idea to build the fence a few inches inside your property line.

Also, remember to check with the local building department about restrictions on height and style. Many communities have local organizations that exert great influence on what you can or cannot build in your yard.

Trees can sometimes present a problem for fence-builders. Attaching a fence to a tree is not good for the fence or the tree. If the tree bark is damaged during the building of the fence, the tree will be more susceptible to disease. And a tree shaking in high winds will damage any solid fence. The solution is to curve the fence around the tree or set it back from the tree.

Fence Materials

The structure of a fence is simple: it is made up of posts, stringers, and infill. But this simple pattern can be varied in myriad ways, depending on your choice of materials.

Posts are commonly made of metal, concrete, or wood. Wood posts have to be of wood that is resistant to decay, such as the heartwood of redwood, cedar, or cypress, or pressure-treated wood. The common practice of painting wood post with creosote

or some other protective chemical actually provides little protection because it only coats the wood with a thin film. Soaking the bottom 18 to 24 inches of posts in a mixture of half creosote and half diesel fuel is much more effective.

Stringers, or the crosspieces between posts, are commonly wood, except on metal fences. The stringers can either be the main design feature of the fence, as in a rail fence, or they can provide support for the infill, such as pickets or upright boards.

The reason that fences vary so greatly in appearance is primarily because of the infill material. Pickets, boards, grapestakes, bamboo, laths, plywood, clapboard: you name it, and you can probably find a fence made of it.

This casual fence is sufficient to divert foot traffic from cutting across this front lawn.

Gates can reflect the personality of the owners, their outlook on life, and their community. Just consider the difference between a high, solid, locked gate, and a rose-entwined gate that doesn't close properly anymore.

One gate says, "You better have a good reason to be here," and the other says, "Come on in, the coffee's still hot."

A gate can also help set the mood to the property, as a beautiful wrought iron gate does when set in the archway entrance to a hacienda.

Gates can be decorative, unobtrusive, or simply utilitarian. Even the harsh appearance of a chain-link gate can be disguised or softened, however, by inserting wood slats through the links.

Whatever type of gate you choose, all have similar components. Review the accompanying drawing of a typical wooden gate, with all its components and hardware. A wide variety of gate hardware is available, from hinges to latches, depending on the style of your gate and fence.

Gates receive frequent use so don't skimp on design, building materials, or hardware. A poor quality gate will constantly remind you of your error.

Design and Construction Considerations

In planning your gate, consider two points: where will it go in the fence line, and which way will it swing? Front gates generally swing inward, like a front door, so guests don't have to back up. An outward-swinging gate near a sidewalk could be a hazard to unsuspecting pedestrians.

Gate Construction

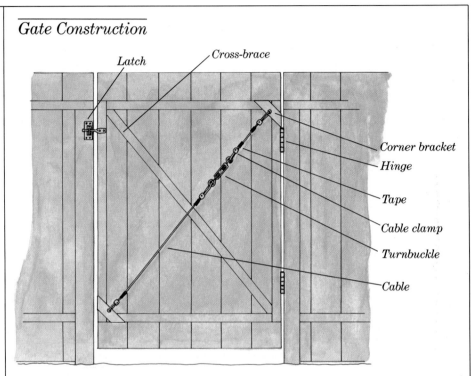

Latch · Cross-brace · Corner bracket · Hinge · Tape · Cable clamp · Turnbuckle · Cable

Above: *This double gate matches the colonial style of the house and picket fence.*

Right: *Don't skimp on a gate's design or quality. This gate provides daily pleasure throughout the year.*

Gates in areas other than the entranceway may swing any way you decide is more practical. If you choose the right hardware, the gate can swing both ways. Some gates don't swing at all, they slide back along the fence—a style often used with extra-wide gates.

When building your own gate, the chief concern is to keep it from sagging. There are two reasons for a sagging gate: the post on which it hangs leans over, or the gate frame sags out of line.

Gate posts are often heavier than the line posts, and may be set in concrete or planted deeper for additional strength.

The gate itself must be built to minimize the possibility of sagging. The standard method is to run a cross-brace inside the gate frame from the bottom of the hinge side to the top of the latch side. This acts like a 45-degree-angle support brace. Running the brace from the bottom of the latch side to the top of the hinge side, which is commonly done, is not really very effective.

A sagging gate frame can also be straightened through the use of a light cable and turnbuckle. Attach strong eye-hooks to the corners opposite the cross-brace at the top of the hinge side and the bottom of the latch side, join a length of cable to each one with a turnbuckle in the middle. Tighten the turnbuckle until the gate frame straightens.

The positioning of the gate is a matter of personal choice, though there are a few practical considerations. The gate should be placed at the most convenient opening in the fence line. If the area has been heavily traveled before you put the fence in, put the gate where people have traditionally walked.

A curved top, wrought-iron hinges, and a custom made latch add a distinctive touch to this redwood gate.

This wrought-iron gate provides security but doesn't block the view in or out of this Spanish-style courtyard.

Another point to consider when positioning the gate is the lay of the land on both sides of the opening. If the ground rises on one side more than on the other, the gate may only open one way without hitting the soil. If this is a problem, see if you can hinge the gate on the other post for better ground clearance.

Materials

While most gates are metal or wood, the variations in materials within that framework are endless. The type of gate you choose will, of course, be linked to the type of fence you have.

Metal Gates. Metal gates generally fall into two categories: ornamental and functional. A wrought-iron gate is ornamental, but will it be compatible with your fence? If you have a wrought-iron fence or a handsome brick wall around your grounds, it probably will be. But if you have a picket fence, you will want to choose a matching picket gate.

Functional metal gates include farm gates and chain-link gates. Chain-link gates have little aesthetic appeal, but farm gates can be quite attractive in the right setting. These gates are usually made of lightweight aluminum or heavier tubular steel. They range in width from 6 to 20 feet; for very wide openings, two gates can be made to meet in the middle, or a supporting wheel can be put under the swinging end.

Wooden Gates. There is no limit other than your imagination to the types of wooden gates. A gate may be a centerpiece at the entry to your property or something more discreet, such as a service entry gate.

When planning a wooden gate, consider whether or not it will be painted. If not, choose a wood that weathers naturally and beautifully, such as the heartwood of cedar or redwood, or pressure-treated pine.

A gate can blend with the fence or it can mark a sharp break in the fence line, a clear indication of where the opening falls. The sort of gate you choose will depend on your fence and your imagination.

Gates can blend with the fence (top) or contrast to indicate where a person (middle) or vehicle (bottom) can easily enter.

GARDEN WALLS

A garden wall can bring a new focus to your yard, even if it is nothing more than a low, curving line of rocks. A wall not only provides a visual boundary, but can divide your garden into areas for distinctly different uses.

In many ways, the great variety of walls reflects the history of distinct areas in this country. The meandering, loosely laid stone walls of New England are a reflection of the ruggedness of the land, and remind us of the difficulties endured by early settlers there while clearing the land for tilling. The high, adobe-plastered walls of the Southwest take their materials from the parched desert lands and recall the colonizers from the south who built walls to enclose elegant courtyards and to screen their homes from the desert winds.

A wall may be nothing more than a few courses of stone or concrete block to mark the edge of a suburban lawn, or it may be a sinuously curving brick wall built by a master craftsman to enclose an estate.

You may want a stone retaining wall, a low brick divider wall, or an open wall of decorative concrete blocks. Since a wall is generally permanent, be sure to reread the section on overall yard design and consider how the wall will fit into your yard before you begin to build.

Top: A loose stone wall is a perfect companion for this planted hillside.

Bottom: This brick retaining wall defines a more formal landscape.

Opposite page: A rustic dry stone wall is full of character and complements any landscape for many years.

When planning a stone or masonry wall, remember that most walls need a concrete footing poured beneath the frost line. Even if you live where the soil does not freeze, you should pour a footing at least 6 inches below the ground surface, and 6 inches thick. A mortared wall that is built without a concrete footing will shift and crack, undoing all your efforts.

The one type of stone wall that does not need a footing is the stone wall laid without mortar. If properly built, it can move with the ground during frost heave and still remain intact. Even with this type of wall, the first layer of rocks should still be stabilized and placed several inches deep in the ground.

Depending on the type of wall you want to build, you may have to obtain building permits and meet local codes. Generally, permits are not required for walls 3 feet or less in height, but if you have any doubt about whether your wall will require a permit, call the building inspector's office. If you are thinking of building a wall across the front of your property to screen your yard from the street, be sure to check first with the building inspector. Most residential areas strictly control the height of front-yard fences and walls.

If you are planning a retaining wall, you must take special care to make it strong. The earth behind the wall, particularly when loaded with water, will exert tremendous pressure on the wall. As a result, retaining walls must have drains built in to let water through, and they must be tied to the footing with reinforcement rods to prevent the wet earth from toppling them.

One type of wall that should not be overlooked is the "living wall" of shrubs, hedges, or closely planted trees. Such living walls are far less obtrusive than stone or brick walls; instead, they appear to be a natural part of the garden. Architecturally neutral, these green walls can be much more inviting than a solid wall, which may often appear forbidding.

Design and Construction Considerations

The scale of a masonry wall must be in balance with the scale of the garden. A 6-foot-high solid masonry wall encircling a small lot will give it a prison-like atmosphere; a lower wall topped with a wooden rail will give the yard a more open feeling.

When topped with a wooden cap, low concrete or brick walls make excellent patio borders and can be used for extra seating.

In addition to scale, be aware of the effect of building materials on the appearance of the wall. Bricks, for instance, are more formal than dry-laid stone walls. Used brick or vines provide a softer effect.

Concrete block walls, while relatively inexpensive and easy to build, have an unpleasant utilitarian appearance. Improve their appearance by using colored, textured, or patterned blocks; by arranging some of the blocks with the cells sideways and making planters out of them; or by inserting decorative blocks at regular intervals along the wall.

Materials define a masonry wall as formal (top) or more casual (bottom).

Materials

When planning a masonry or stone wall, you should first visit masonry yards in your area to see what is available. A good masonry yard will have many types of concrete block, decorative block, and stone.

Here are some of the materials you should find in your masonry yard:

Concrete Block. The most economical type of masonry wall is the one built with basic concrete blocks. These blocks come in standard 6- or 8-inch widths, and are 8 inches high and 16 inches long. The actual dimensions are ⅜ inch smaller in every direction to allow for the ⅜-inch mortar joint between the blocks. There are also 8-inch-square blocks, called half-blocks, which are used at the ends of walls.

In addition to the standard building blocks, you should also be able to find decorative concrete blocks. An entire wall can be built with these decorative blocks, or they can be interspersed in a solid wall or used for a border.

While concrete block walls generally appear mundane and functional, they can be readily disguised by painting them or covering them with two layers of stucco. The second coat of stucco has a powdered color mixed with the stucco to match or contrast with the color of your house.

More expensive than standard concrete block, but also much more visually appealing, are slump block, which resembles adobe, and split-face block, which looks like cut stone.

Brick. Brick remains a standard material for garden walls, valued for its durability and flexibility of design. Bricks can be laid on end, set on edge, or turned to create an endless variety of patterns. Design variations can also be achieved by using bricks of different colors or textures.

Most brick walls are actually composed of two parallel brick walls, with the mortar joints on one side offset by the distance of half a brick on the other side for greater strength.

Brick walls take considerably more time to build than concrete block walls—in double-wall construction, it takes 16 bricks to match the size of one concrete block—but the end result is generally more attractive.

In addition to taking more time, the great number of bricks required adds to the expense of building brick walls. As a result, you may want to limit brick projects to planter walls or low divider walls.

Concrete Block Wall

Reinforcing steel

Concrete footing

Brick Wall

Reinforcing steel

Concrete footing

Rough bricks, painted wood, and colored decorative blocks combine to form a classy wall.

Mortared Stone Wall

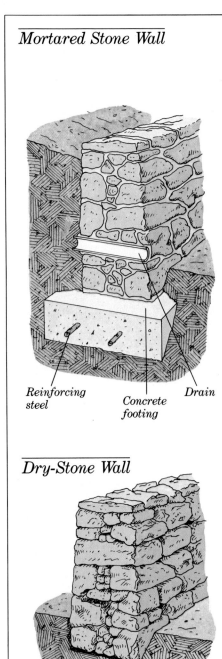

Reinforcing steel *Concrete footing* *Drain*

Dry-Stone Wall

Soil *Stone footing*

Stone. If you live in an area with a plentiful supply of exposed natural stone, you can create stone walls in and around your garden just for the price of hauling the stone. If not, buy stone at a masonry yard.

You can build a stone wall using mortar to hold the stone in place or without mortar. If you don't use mortar, position the stones so their weight holds them in place. There is a considerable amount of heavy labor to a stone wall. Work at your own pace. Stones must be carefully selected and placed to prevent the end result from looking like a pile of rocks. Spread the stones on the ground and pick through them to find the best fit.

There are two basic types of stone: quarried stone and fieldstone. Quarried stone, such as marble, is cut from a mountainside, and this labor dramatically raises the price.

Fieldstone is rock found along streams or in fields. It is available in two versions: rubble and roughly squared stone. Rubble is natural rock; roughly squared stone has been shaped with a hammer and chisel. You can buy roughly squared rock, or make it yourself, as described on page 86.

Broken Concrete. This material makes an excellent low retaining wall that is not only attractive but easy to construct. If you find an area where concrete is being torn up, such as a city block or playground where the paving is being replaced, you can probably have all the broken concrete you want just for the asking. Flat and of the same thickness, you just stack it as you do with bricks, overlapping joints wherever you can. The rough, exposed face, full of gravel, gives the wall the rugged look of an old stone wall.

Plants. The living wall of trees or hedges takes much longer to "construct" than other walls, but when grown it is truly a part of your garden. The plants you choose and the way you plant them will determine the appearance of the living wall. Conifers can grow into a dense wall, whereas a line of espaliered fruit trees will provide an open, airy effect. A hedge can be densely-planted or pruned for a more open look.

A high brick wall provides privacy and reduces noise.

*Depending on the design
goals, garden walls can blend
(top) or contrast (bottom) with
the rest of the landscape.*

SHADE STRUCTURES

*I*n many parts of the country, your patio or deck may be too hot to enjoy during the summer. The solution is to build a shade structure that will protect you from the sun's rays while allowing you to enjoy the garden.

Shade structures come in several styles, and are sometimes known by different names in different parts of the country. These include the gazebo or belvedere, pergola or arbor, summer house or garden house, lath house, and the Southwest's ramada.

In addition to providing sun protection, shade structures add a new element to the garden. They offer a sense of protective enclosure, define a portion of the outdoor room, protect shade-loving plants, and support climbing vines.

A shade structure can serve several purposes at one time, and can be modified as a family's needs change. It may be a sandbox and tricycle area for preschoolers during the day and a haven for adults in the evening. Adding a table makes it usable for hobbies and games. Add some stereo equipment and it's an excellent party room for teenagers.

These shade structures may be attached to the existing house, or freestanding. You may even want both types. If your patio or deck extends from the house, all or part of it may be shaded by a structure attached to the eaves. At the same time, a gazebo or garden house can offer temporary sanctuary from the confusion of the house and family.

Shade structures can be ideal for growing plants (top), define "rooms" in a patio or deck (middle), or provide much needed shade on hot summer days.

The roofs of shade structures are generally open, since they are principally designed to provide shade rather than protection from rain. But this is not always the case. In areas where intense heat is not a problem, the structure may provide only the suggestion of a covering from spaced beams overhead. In other areas, the roof may be completely covered for protection against both sun and rain.

In addition to the large-scale shade structures described above, your house may benefit from simple shade devices over west-facing windows. One such device is the cantilevered eyebrow that extends the roof line to shade a window or wall. This works in much the same manner as a canvas awning, but by using wood, the addition can be made to more closely follow the lines of the house.

Always check local building codes to see if a permit is required. Some codes say that a shade structure of 400 square feet or less does not require a permit. However, any building you add to your property must be structurally sound and must meet local setback rules.

Design and Construction Considerations

Shade structures in the garden can be roofed solidly or covered just enough to diffuse direct sunlight. They can be elaborate garden living rooms or simple sheltered nooks. Most are built as freestanding structures, but they can also be built along an existing wall or fence.

The design of your shade structure should blend with the overall design of your garden. For instance, you would not be likely to put a rough-timbered ramada typical of the Southwest in a formal New England garden, but the ramada would be appropriate in an arid setting.

More elaborate shade structures can be covered or enclosed with the same materials used for patio roofs.

Some other considerations become important when you are planning a structure with enclosed sides: How much air circulation do you need? Do you want to create real privacy or just a sense of privacy? Do you want year-round shade or only summer shade? Thoughtful choice of design and materials is important.

The garden house shade structure can serve many different functions. It can include outdoor cooking and dining facilities, or it can house an attractively enclosed tool shed and potting area. It can shelter a hot tub, with part or all of it serving as a dressing room. You can also design a garden house that serves as a simple retreat from the sun and a vantage point for viewing the garden.

The addition of shade structures makes these outdoor living areas a feature attraction.

Shade Structures

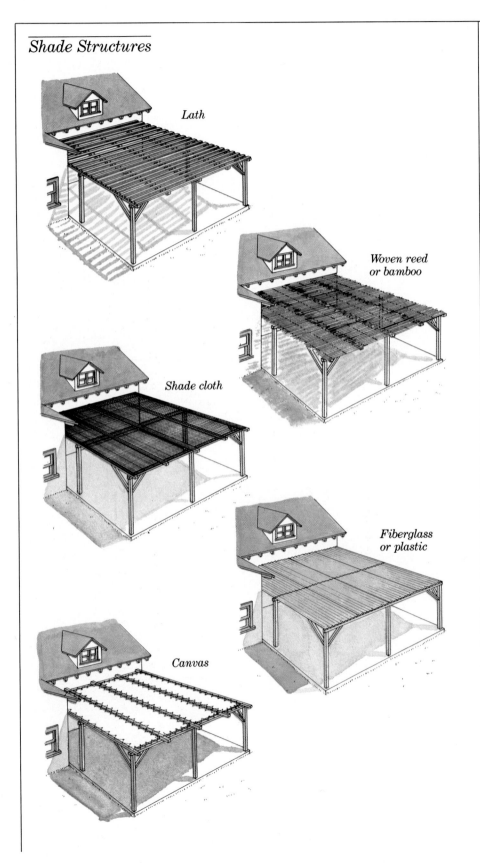

Lath

Woven reed or bamboo

Shade cloth

Fiberglass or plastic

Canvas

If you live in an area with mosquitoes, consider screening the shade structure. It will make those hot summer nights much more pleasant, and the screens will keep out pesky flies.

The appearance and usefulness of a shade structure can be altered in many ways. A garden house can be made to seem more solid by adding louvered wooden panels, for instance. Container plants or hanging baskets can brighten a pergola and link it with the garden. You may even want to think about wiring your shade structure to provide electricity for lights, music, or a fan.

Attached Shade Structures

Attached shade structures have the double advantage of being strongly supported by the house and eliminating the need for about half the support posts. As a result, they are much easier to build.

Nevertheless, these structures should be built securely and should be strong enough to support a couple hundred pounds just in case you want to add a roof later. The overhead beams should slope slightly downward from the house so rainwater will run off if you do add a roof. A drop of ¼ inch per foot is generally sufficient.

There are dozens of different styles of shade coverings. A common style of attached overhang is made with 4 by 4 posts spaced 8 feet apart, topped by a 4 by 6 beam, with rafters extending from the eaves to the beam. Shade is provided by topping the rafters with the material of your choice, from redwood 2 by 2s to bamboo screens.

The overall impact of your shade structure will be enhanced by attention to details in the design. Note how the ends of rafters and beams on some of the shade structures have been shaped in different designs. This is a time-consuming job but one that will earn you many compliments.

Opposite page: *Additional shade can increase the livability of outdoor spaces.*

If you need sun protection for part of the year and openness for the remainder of the year, you will want to build removable shade panels. Alternatively, you can put up bamboo screens or the shade cloths used by nurseries to protect their outdoor plants. They can be rolled up or removed when you don't need them.

In gardens that receive little direct sunlight, open beams will lend a sense of protection and comfort to the patio or deck without actually interfering with light.

Freestanding Shade Structures

Freestanding shade structures come in numerous styles, from the heavy-framed solidity of the pergola or ramada to the lacy delicacy of a Victorian gazebo.

Freestanding structures require a minimum of four posts in two rows. If space is available, a rectangular form with six posts is more attractive because it is a step beyond the simple, basic box.

Shear bracing in two directions is needed to keep these structures from swaying. The bracing can be 45-degree-angle knee braces or heavy steel T-braces attached where post and beam meet.

Here are some typical freestanding shade structures to consider.

■ The gazebo is the classic shade structure. It can be a Victorian design reminiscent of a romantic novel or a contemporary design of your choosing. Kits are available in square, hexagonal, or octagonal forms.

■ The ramada, first built by cowboys for protection from the hot Southwest sun, was made of whatever material could be found. Today's versions are usually made of large, rough-cut timbers, topped with palm fronds, reed stalks, or narrow sticks.

■ The lath house differs from other shade structures because it is designed more for shading plants than for protecting people. But you'd be wise to make yours large enough to accommodate a table and chairs because you and guests will inevitably gravitate there.

Shade Structures

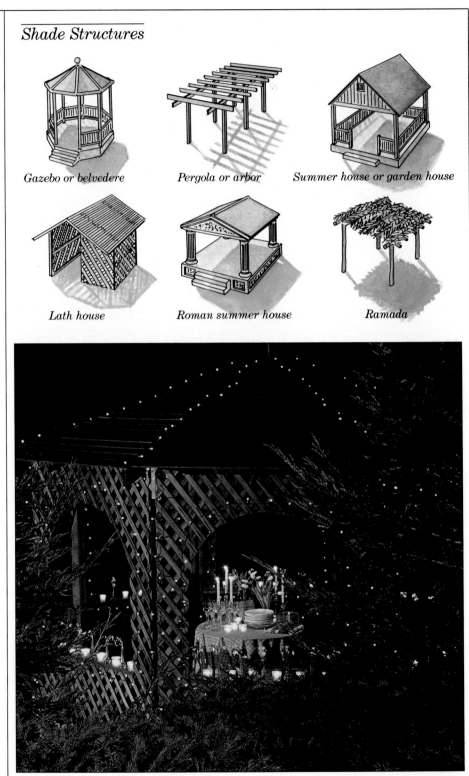

Gazebo or belvedere

Pergola or arbor

Summer house or garden house

Lath house

Roman summer house

Ramada

A gazebo becomes an even better place for entertaining with the addition of low-voltage outdoor lighting.

■ The garden house is generally rectangular and is simpler to build than the gazebo. It doubles as a shade structure for plants and a quiet entertainment spot.

Materials

The materials used in your shade structure will depend on the design you choose. A rugged ramada naturally calls for rough-hewn poles, while a Victorian gazebo is made with smooth wood.

Any poles or posts that are in touch with the ground must be made of heartwood of redwood or cedar, or be pressure-treated, to resist decay. Similarly, any wood that will be left natural, rather than being painted or stained, should be soaked in a clear water repellant.

Plan your project carefully on paper before starting to build; it will save you hours of running back and forth to the lumberyard for material you overlooked.

Flooring. Shade structures can have floors of wood, concrete, stone, brick, tile, or gravel. Gravel, however, is practical only if the seats are stationary.

Covering. The density of the shade under the finished structure is determined by the material, and the spacing of the material, used for the roofing. The rafters themselves may be covering enough if vines are trained over the top. For both summer shade and winter sun, the material should be removable.

Rolls of woven reed or bamboo can be installed or removed quickly. They create a pleasant, mottled shade, and are reasonably priced, but they will not last more than a couple summers.

Shade cloth used to protect outdoor plants comes in a range of densities. Depending on the tightness of the weave, the cloth will screen from 30 to 90 percent of the sunlight. When putting it in place, be sure to leave a slight billow to allow for shrinkage. Shade cloth is easy to remove and roll up for winter storage.

Instead of making the patio roof of wood or plastic, consider planting vines to create a bower. Some vines are fast-growing and provide shade within a season.

In addition to adding beauty to a garden, vines soften the outline of a shade structure and create more shade. Many vines flower each year, and some produce fragrant flowers, while others produce edible fruit. All can shelter an area from the wind and create privacy.

If you are thinking of adding vines to your shade structure, consider using deciduous vines, which lose their leaves in the winter, or evergreen vines. Deciduous vines reflect the seasons, while evergreens give year-round protection. The evergreen should be considered only in mild climates without severe winter frosts.

Shade material includes 2 by 2s (top), plastic cloth (middle), and woven reed (bottom).

STORAGE SHEDS

*S*ometimes it seems as though someone forgot that "home" means outdoor as well as indoor activities. Outdoor activities, frequently accompanied by heavy or bulky equipment, require additional storage space.

Hundreds of large and small items must be kept in some kind of order. Yet your home may have no outdoor storage area. Or its storage area may have no closets, cabinets, or shelves. This section will help you find solutions to these problems.

Although most people think of a shed simply as a place to store tools—or a lot of junk you can't bear to throw away—it can be much more versatile. You could have a small shed to hide a garbage can, or a potting shed attached to the back of your house, or a firewood shelter.

This clever storage area provides work space, shade, and plenty of storage space.

Before you choose a shed, consider its uses, and then buy or build for your specific needs. One word of advice here: if it's going to be a garden shed or a potting shed, make it twice as big as you think you'll actually need. You will always need more space.

The basic garden shed can be turned into much more than a simple storage unit; put a deck around it and a trellis overhead and it becomes a pool cabana or a child's playhouse, or virtually anything you design it to be. It can also easily become a great place to put guests when your house overflows, especially with a batch of kids home on vacation.

The shed should meet three requirements: it fits your overall storage plan, it only consumes the money, time, and effort you wish to invest, and its structural design and appearance are appropriate for your site.

Types of Sheds

The three basic types of sheds are prefabricated metal, wood kits, or a wood shed you build to your own specifications. The latter case would assume you are a reasonably accomplished carpenter. At any rate, refer to Ortho's books *Basic Carpentry Techniques* and *Outdoor Storage*.

Materials

In a metal shed, you can choose from aluminum or painted steel. With a wood shed, the prefabricated models generally have plywood walls, but you can alter that by putting up additional siding material such as shingles or something to match the siding on your house.

Because the metal and wood materials differ in their structural capabilities, the disparate types will vary in looks, ease of modification, and time required for assembly. For example, metal sheds are easier to put up and are fairly standardized in form. The main differences among models are in sizes, roof styles, and features such as door-closing systems

and protective finishes. By contrast, erecting a wood shed is a more complex process that requires more building skills. But wood sheds are also relatively simple to customize, and to expand.

Another key advantage to wood sheds is that they can be easily insulated, which metal sheds cannot. The insulation bats are stapled between the studs and rafters and then covered with dry wall or paneling.

Adding insulation and drywall is a lot more work, but this adaptability to insulation is critical in cold climates.

While a small metal shed can be put up in a few hours, a large do-it-yourself wood shed may take a week or more. So before you jump into one of these projects, make an honest appraisal of your skill and your time available. It may be worth it to you to have someone else build it.

Shed Construction

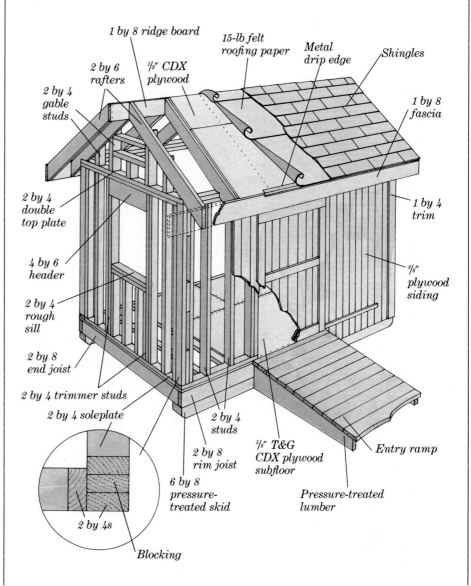

1 by 8 ridge board

2 by 6 rafters

2 by 4 gable studs

½" CDX plywood

15-lb felt roofing paper

Metal drip edge

Shingles

1 by 8 fascia

2 by 4 double top plate

1 by 4 trim

4 by 6 header

⅜" plywood siding

2 by 4 rough sill

2 by 8 end joist

2 by 4 trimmer studs

2 by 4 soleplate

2 by 4 studs

2 by 8 rim joist

6 by 8 pressure-treated skid

⅝" T&G CDX plywood subfloor

Entry ramp

Pressure-treated lumber

2 by 4s

Blocking

If you choose a kit, check the instructions carefully. Some are easy to build, others are little more than a stack of lumber. No matter what type of kit you select—or if you build your own—some site preparation will be required.

Many sheds do not include a foundation or floor—often the same thing since they expect you to put it on a concrete slab—in the price. You can also put a shed on redwood or treated wood boards and then fill the interior with pea gravel for a simple floor on level ground.

Whatever you choose, strike a balance between cost and attractiveness. If later you decide it is too small or unattractive, replacing it will cost twice as much as the original.

Design and Construction Considerations

With a prefabricated metal shed, what you see is what you get. But with a wooden structure that you design and build, or have built, there are countless variations available. The roofing and siding material can be anything you wish, and you can readily add skylights, customized windows, and special trim. Here are some of the major considerations:

■ Codes and permits. Check with your local building department about what permits will be required. In many areas, sheds with less than 120 square feet do not need permits.

■ Cost. Prices range roughly from $100 to $700, with wood sheds costing more than metal ones. Site preparation and any materials not included in the prefabricated packages—such as a floor—will run the price up.

■ Siting. The place you choose to put the shed will affect how large your shed can be, how easy it will be to erect, how convenient it will be to use, and how durable it will be.

■ Appearance. Any new structure in your yard will be part of your life for a long time, so do your best to match the shed's style and color with your house.

Wood sheds can be custom built to specific styes (top) or purposes (bottom).

■ Climate. All kinds of weather affect a building, so pick a structural design that is appropriate to your climate. A metal shed in particular is vulnerable to damage from strong winds, snow, or salt air. Metal sheds are also difficult to insulate.

Size

Another important thing to keep in mind is the scale of your shed. If you are using a prefab, check the overall height before buying it and see how it will look in your yard.

If you are building your own, plan on cutting the studs down below the standard 92¼-inch height. In fact, if you cut them 86 inches long and then use 2 by 6s for door and window headers, the headers will still be the standard 80 inches above the sill, but your building will appear lower and more in tune with the garden. A standard height structure that is only 10 by 12 looks too high, and out of proportion.

Roof, Walls, and Openings

Other considerations are the type of roof and the placement of doors, windows, and interior walls, since they will affect access and storage capacity. In all but the metal prefabs, the repositioning of doors and windows is relatively easy.

Roof style. In considering a shed, pay careful attention to the different roof styles, since that is probably the most distinctive feature. You will be able to choose between the standard gable, the barn-like gambrel, the sloping shed roof, or the geodesic dome style.

Interior walls. If your shed is to serve more than one purpose, interior walls can help it do so. Interior walls define space and separate activity areas that you don't want to mix. For example, you could run a solid wall through the middle of the shed and place a door to the outside at each end of the structure to create a playhouse for the kids on one side that is restricted from the tools and paint on the other side.

Interior walls can be put anywhere you like, since they are partitions and not walls that carry the roof's weight.

Doors and windows. Having doors and windows in the right place is important because it determines how you enter the shed and where you get your light. Doors and windows can go wherever you wish as long as they are properly framed. Door placement can also affect movement inside the shed. Experiment with plans to see what style would best suit your needs.

Skylights are a plus in any shed, as are clerestory windows in traditional shed styles, because they allow ample light without using up valuable wall space. They also aid in security because strangers cannot readily see what is inside. A burglar doesn't want to climb a ladder just to see what you have inside your shed.

Upgrading Existing Sheds

A plain shed can be given a dramatic facelift by adding such things as decking or a patio around it, or by attaching a shade structure. So all of a sudden instead of just having a tool shed, it is now a pool cabana, an outdoor kitchen, or a playhouse.

A dark and musty shed, which one often becomes, can be brightened with the addition of a skylight or two in the roof. Skylights sound intimidating but are relatively easy to put in on roofs covered with asbestos shingles, wood shingles, or shakes, particularly if installed before the roofing material is applied.

If you have a typical sloping shed roof already built on your grounds, you can alter it by adding a row of clerestory windows along the top and a porch roof in front. Now you have something that looks like a small guest house.

Storage areas can be obvious like this metal shed (top) or hidden behind walls (bottom).

Storing Tools and Equipment

If all of your garden tools are already neatly in their proper places, you needn't read this. If, however, you are among us lesser mortals, here are some simple but effective means of organizing garden tools.

Long-handled tools often seem to be the most bothersome, but they can easily be hung from a long 2 by 4 nailed to the wall of the storage area. Drive nails in pairs as shown to support each tool. For a more finished appearance, use wood dowels set at a slight upward angle instead of nails. When drilling the dowel holes, use a drilling template made from a block of wood to keep the angles the same.

The storage capacity can be doubled by placing two boards across the wall, one above the other, then staggering the hanging tools.

Boards that will be installed in a wood frame structure can be nailed to the studs. If mounting the boards on a masonry wall, first drill holes with a masonry bit, then place expansion shields in the holes for the mounting lag bolts.

Equipment that is not used frequently can be handily stored overhead by making a rack out of 1 by 4s with a sheet of ¾-inch plywood as the platform. Assemble the two lumber slings as shown then nail to the exposed joists or collar ties in your storage area.

Few items will help you get organized better than a lot of shelves. You have to have somewhere to put all that junk you have collected. Simple storage shelves can be made from 1 by 12 wood, ¾-inch plywood, or ¾-inch particle board. Keep the shelf length at 3 feet or less to prevent sagging.

A shelf like the one illustrated is basically made by cutting the two side pieces to the length you want, then cutting two pieces for the top and bottom and gluing and nailing them between the two side pieces.

Hooks and Racks

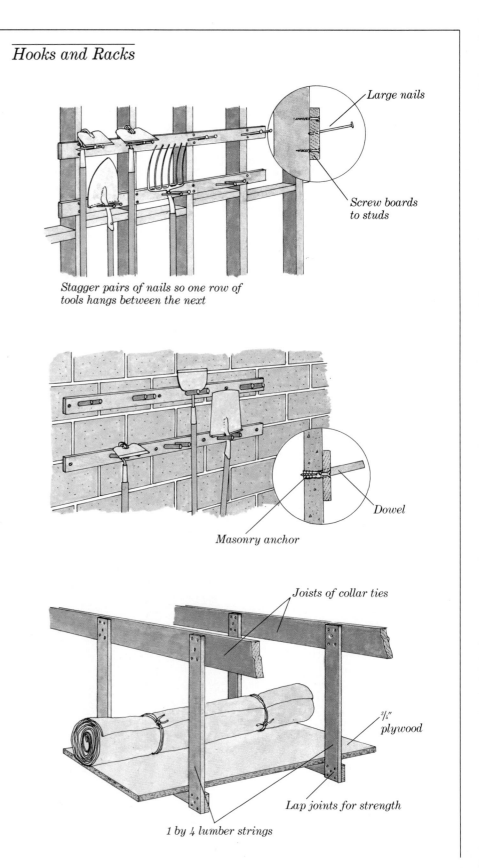

Stagger pairs of nails so one row of tools hangs between the next

Large nails

Screw boards to studs

Masonry anchor

Dowel

Joists of collar ties

¾" plywood

Lap joints for strength

1 by 4 lumber strings

But before you do that, install two shelf tracks inside the side pieces. For a finished appearance the tracks can be inset by cutting grooves for them with a router, or you can simply screw them to the side pieces.

Put the elongated box together now with glue and nails. A freestanding shelf like this would not be rigid enough to stand up straight. It should be attached to the wall with nailing strips. So lay the shelf face down and measure the diagonals. When they are equal, the box is square. Inset a 1 by 4 nailing strip into the side pieces at the top and bottom and glue and nail it in place.

Raise the shelf against the wall and attach it to the wall by nailing through the nailing strips into the studs. Make sure you have squared it again before you do this.

Now measure the distance between the shelf tracks, cut the shelves to fit, and hang them on the shelf supports.

An even faster and easier way to put up simple shelves for garden supplies and small tools is to attach shelf tracks directly to the studs and then use 12-inch shelf brackets to support the shelf material. For maximum support, place a shelf track and bracket over each stud in the area you wish to cover with shelves.

Storage Shelves

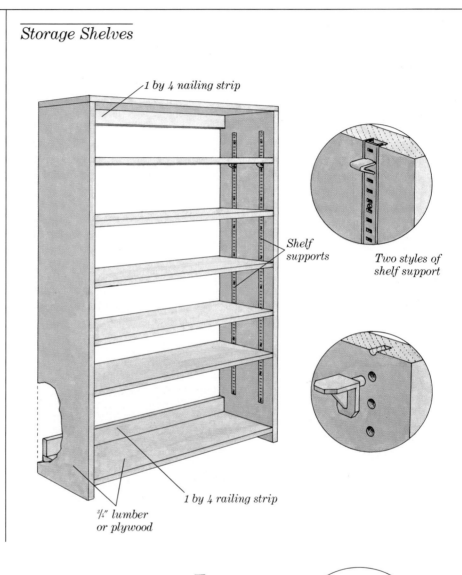

1 by 4 nailing strip

Shelf supports

Two styles of shelf support

1 by 4 railing strip

¾" lumber or plywood

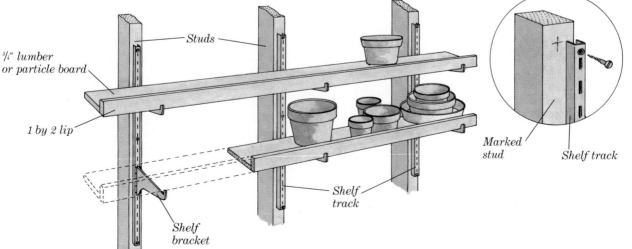

¾" lumber or particle board

Studs

1 by 2 lip

Shelf bracket

Shelf track

Marked stud

Shelf track

OTHER GARDEN PROJECTS

On the next four pages, you will find information to help you design and plan other garden projects including lawn edging, raised planting beds, compost bins, trellises, and attached greenhouses.

Lawn Edging

If you have a flower bed next to a lawn, you know the problems you have trying to keep the grass out of the flowers. Lawn edging prevents this sort of problem and creates a sharply defined border for your lawn.

Edging, which can be made from many different materials, should be sunk into the ground about 4 inches to prevent grass roots from spreading underneath. The top of the edging is usually placed flush with the surface so that a lawn mower can pass over it. This eliminates the chore of clipping along the edge of a raised border.

Borders can range from the simple plastic edging strips available in most hardware stores to concrete edging topped with brick. An attractive, long-lasting edging can also be made with lengths of 2 by 4 decay-resistant lumber, landscape timbers, or old railroad ties set into the ground.

Raised Planting Beds

If you are gardening in a small space, few designs succeed like raised planting beds. Even if you have a large garden, consider converting all or part of it into raised beds. The advantages are numerous: weeds are more easily controlled, compost can be readily added and worked into the soil, and plastic covers can be fitted over the beds for an earlier start in the spring and for frost protection in the fall.

Top: Brick (left) and rot-resistant wood (right) are common edging materials.

Bottom: A raised planting bed makes gardening easier.

Raised beds are commonly made from 2 by 12 rough, decay-resistant lumber. Handsome raised beds can also be built out of stacked railroad ties, 4 by 4s, or even concrete blocks.

You can turn the raised beds into comfortable garden seats by screwing 2 by 6s to the tops of 2 by 12 borders. These seats also make weeding less tiring.

If you have an old window or two lying around, put them to use as the tops of cold frames. Under the protective glass, you can start plants weeks ahead of schedule for transplanting into the garden after frost danger has passed.

Compost Bins

Good compost is as precious as caviar to the fervent gardener. Almost anything will do: leaves, vegetable refuse from the kitchen, egg shells, grass clippings, straw, and even coffee grounds and shredded paper. The objective is to turn this waste material into rich, dark soil through the use of compost bins.

Compost must be piled in a particular way and provided with adequate ventilation, so that soil bacteria can thrive and break down the waste. Bacteria need moisture, air, and food.

Gardeners have found that a series of layers of waste material with fertilizers, manures, and garden soil between the layers makes the best compost pile.

The size of your compost pile will depend on the size of your garden. But two 4 by 6 piles are easier to handle than one 4 by 12 pile. Better yet are three 4 by 4 piles, with new compost starting on one side, developing compost in the middle, and finishing compost on the other end.

The bin shown will hold generous amounts of compost and is designed to provide the air circulation so important for proper decomposition. View the job as four dividers which are held sturdily by the boards across the back and by the pipe reinforcement at the front.

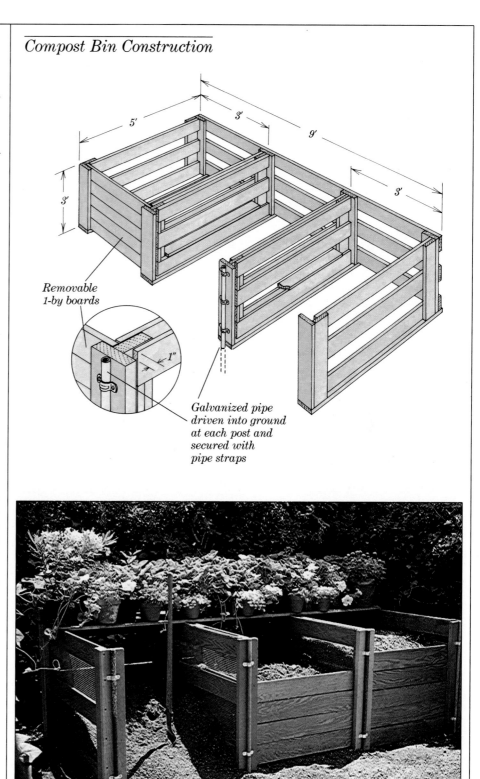

Compost Bin Construction

Removable 1-by boards

Galvanized pipe driven into ground at each post and secured with pipe straps

Compost bins are easy to build and produce excellent mulch and soil conditioner.

Garden Trellises

A garden trellis can bring back memories of *Wisteria* by the back porch, or cool grapes hanging from the vine.

Espaliered plants and vines require a sturdy frame or trellis to grow on. If the plant foliage is heavy, it can be attractive on a trellis of very simple design; if the plants are light and delicate, the trellis structure itself may become the focal point of the design.

A standard trellis is built of 2 by 2 lumber, which is strong enough to support vines yet light enough to give the trellis an airy appearance. Bolt the 2 by 2s (using rust-resistant connectors) directly to the wall of your house or shed. Vertical 2 by 2s spaced 16 inches apart, or over the house studs, are then used to support the crosspieces that form the lattice.

The 2 by 2s can be painted or stained to match the color of the house, making them nearly invisible behind the plants. Because the plants are held away from the house, they will provide shade while allowing air circulation next to the house.

Another way to build a trellis against a house is to bolt the uprights to the overhanging rafter tails. Put two 2 by 2s on each rafter for a balanced look. Add crosspieces as desired. The advantage of this system is that no part of the trellis is directly in contact with the house siding. The trellis can be taken down in the winter by simply unbolting the vertical pieces from the rafters.

When building your own trellis, it is a good idea to make it larger than you think it needs to be, so that it will support the fully-grown vines without appearing weak and frail.

Hanging Trellis

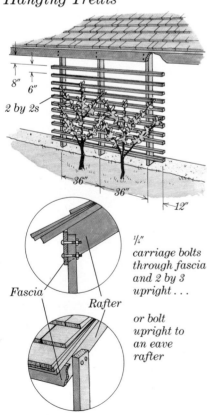

8"
6"
2 by 2s

36"
36"
12"

Fascia
Rafter

¼" carriage bolts through fascia and 2 by 3 upright . . .

or bolt upright to an eave rafter

Arbors can add grace and beauty, as well as shade, to a garden. Woody vines need strong support.

Attached Greenhouse

There are many types of greenhouses, but the attached greenhouse offers significant advantages over others. First, it is easier to build than a freestanding style because construction starts from a fixed wall. Second, the attached greenhouse can be heated from the house, or it can become a solar catchment to help heat the main house. Finally, it is easy to reach regardless of the weather.

Before you build a greenhouse, ask yourself these questions:

■ How big a greenhouse do I need? The answer from greenhouse growers is nearly unanimous: Make it bigger than you think necessary, because once you start using it, you will want to expand.

■ Do I want a prefab or do I want to build my own? Consider both the time and the money you have available. If you want to build your own but think you are too inexperienced, you may want to hire someone to work with you.

■ How much will it cost to heat and cool? The greenhouse will have to be heated in winter and kept cool in the summer. However, greenhouses equipped with solar heat sinks, such as barrels of water, will need little or no additional heat in the winter. Be sure the greenhouse has adequate ventilation, including an overhead fan, to keep it cool in the summer.

■ Will I need a building permit? Be sure that any greenhouse you build meets setback requirements.

■ What covering do you want to use? Factors to consider include cost, ease of construction, permanence, and your own aesthetic sense. Glass remains a top choice because it is attractive, highly resistant to scratching when cleaning, and allows in maximum light. A close second is fiberglass, which is virtually unbreakable, allows in ample light, and is easy to use. When you buy fiberglass, be sure to ask for greenhouse fiberglass, which is specially treated to prevent darkening in a few years.

Attached Greenhouse Construction

Metal joist hanger

Ledger board

Vent

Rafter

Top plate

Studs

Door

Vent

Bottom plate

Overlap corrugated sheets

Nail on ridges

Overhang 2", front and sides

Butt siding sheets at studs

Bead of sealant in joints

Half-round

Corrugated molding

2 by 4 fillers

Cover joint with redwood or cedar lath

An attached greenhouse allows year-round gardening.

CONSTRUCTION TECHNIQUES

This book is primarily an idea book. The first two sections have presented the basic concepts of garden design, along with photographs designed to suggest ways in which you can improve your yard and garden. This section moves into the details of garden construction work. It will tell you what materials to look for, how to estimate your needs, what tools you should have, and what techniques you will need to know to work with wood, brick, stone, and concrete.

This section is also designed to help you understand the aesthetic values of different materials, and how they will look in your particular garden setting. There are many different species of wood, and many different grades of wood among the species. Similarly, there is a wide variety of bricks for your patio planning, and an endless number of patterns to consider when laying that patio. The same is true of stone and concrete.

In this section, you'll also find specifics on how to estimate the amount of materials you will need and how to place orders. Using these guidelines during the planning stages before you start that big project will save you time, money, and hours of frustration.

Although you will probably buy new material for most of your projects, keep your eyes open for used and recycled materials. Not only will they cost less (they may even be free for the hauling), they will already have the patina of age valued by so many landscapers and gardeners.

Most garden construction projects are within the capabilities of the weekend do-it-yourselfer.

Wood used in garden construction can be divided into two general categories: wood that will come in contact with the ground, and wood that will not touch the ground.

Wood that will come in contact with the ground must be either a pressure-treated wood or the heartwood of redwood, cedar, or cypress. If it is one of these species, but is not heartwood, it will soon rot.

Wood used for other garden construction projects is generally of fir or pine. The type depends, in part, on where you live. Throughout much of the country, the wood used for construction is Douglas fir or hemlock; since the two grow together and are similar, this lumber is often called hem-fir. Douglas fir or hem-fir is strong and relatively light, which makes it one of the top choices in the country for construction.

Another excellent species for construction is southern pine. Like fir, it is relatively light and strong, but is sold predominantly in the South.

Pine is widely available across the country, but with the exception of southern pine, it is considered too soft and weak to be used for supporting members in construction. Instead it is commonly used for finish work, such as siding, cabinets, shelves, and door trim. This is because pine can be painted or stained more easily than fir.

Grades of Lumber

Lumber is graded under the direction of several independent agencies located in different regions of the country. The purpose of grading is to give buyers a reliable yardstick by which to measure the quality of lumber. Strength and appearance are the basic criteria for grading.

Lumberyards are fascinating. Comparing prices of different lumber grades can save you money.

Lumber Grading Stamp

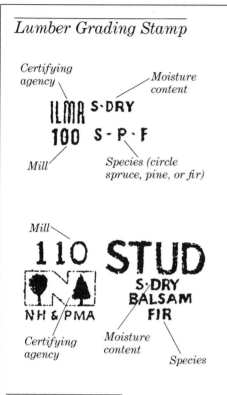

Certifying agency
Moisture content
ILMA S·DRY
100 S · P · F
Mill
Species (circle spruce, pine, or fir)

Mill
110 STUD
S·DRY
BALSAM
FIR
NH & PMA
Certifying agency
Moisture content
Species

Softwood Lumber

There are two major grades of soft-wood lumber. (Hardwoods, used almost exclusively in finish or cabinet-work construction, are not discussed here.) The two grades are *common,* which is graded primarily for structural strength, and *select,* which is graded primarily for appearance rather than strength. Select is used for cabinetwork or paneling and common is used for construction.

Select. Select lumber is divided into four grades, A through D, in descending quality. Grade A is completely free of knots, while grade D has many knots.

Common. Common lumber is used primarily in frame construction. It is broken into four major categories: *select structural, structural joists and planks, light framing lumber,* and *stud grade.*

For most purposes, you need only know something about light framing lumber, which is the most widely used category of lumber for general construction. It is sold in three grades: *construction grade,* which is

the top of the line, *standard grade,* which is almost as good as construction grade but markedly cheaper, and *utility grade,* which is low-quality lumber not suitable for framing work.

Building codes ordinarily require that lumber used in construction be of standard grade or better.

The other common lumber grade is *stud grade,* which is used in building frame studs. It is generally quite straight, which helps the builder put up a straight wall, and is limited to lengths of 10 feet or less. You can buy *precut studs* that are already cut to the standard length of 92¼ inches.

Green. Much of the lumber you buy will be *green,* meaning it is freshly cut and milled. Green lumber contains a high percentage of moisture, making it heavy and subject to warping and twisting if it dries too quickly. This lumber should be nailed in place without delay, or stacked in the shade with sticks between the boards so it can dry more slowly.

Air-dried. Air-dried lumber is much easier to work with. You may occasionally find it stacked in sheds, where it is drying, but most lumberyards don't want to keep large inventories on hand, so they try to sell green lumber, instead.

Kiln-dried. Kiln-dried lumber is used for finish work, such as floors, ceilings, or trim work. This wood has been carefully dried to minimize shrinkage and twisting. Kiln-dried lumber costs more than either green or air-dried lumber.

Lumber must be stamped as green, air-dried, or kiln-dried.

Plywood

Plywood comes in different grades, which are indicated by two or three letters stamped on each sheet. The letters range from A to D and reflect quality. The first letter is for the best face of the plywood, the second letter for the back of the plywood. If there is a third letter, X, the plywood is exterior grade, meaning that the glue that binds the sheets of wood together will not deteriorate when wet.

Plywood Grading Stamp

Grade of face veneer
Grade of back veneer
A - C
Span index
24 / 16 (APA)
Type
EXTERIOR
PS·1·82 102
Mill
Product standard of manufacturer
American Plywood Association trademark

Sizes of Lumber

In a sawmill, the sawyer sizes up each log to determine what type of lumber can be cut from it. A typical log produces the following cuts:

Dimension lumber is 2 to 4 inches thick and 2 or more inches wide. It is used in all types of construction. Dimension lumber is graded for strength rather than appearance.

Boards, which are 1 inch thick, come in all widths up to 12 inches. They are generally used for cabinets, shelves, crates, or exterior siding. Boards are normally graded for appearance rather than strength.

Timbers and beams are 5 by 5 inches or larger and are mostly used for supporting framework. While generally graded for strength, they can also be graded for appearance—to be used in exposed-beam ceilings, for example.

Lumber cut from a log is called *rough* and is measured according to the *actual size.* This means a 2 by 4 measures a full 2 inches by 4 inches. Before it goes to the lumberyard it is surfaced. This smoothing process reduces the size of lumber. Thus, a 2 by 4 rough board measures the full, or *nominal,* 2 by 4 inches. After surfacing, the size, called the *actual* size, measures 1½ inches by 3½ inches. Lumber is always referred to by its nominal size at a lumber yard.

Plywood is the other major type of wood you may buy. A standard sheet is 4 by 8 feet, but it also comes in 9-foot and 10-foot lengths. Standard thicknesses are: ⅜ inch, ½ inch, ⅝ inch, ¾ inch, and 1⅛ inch, which is used for flooring over 4-foot spans. For siding, choose either ⅜ inch, ½ inch, or ⅝ inch thickness. The heavier the plywood, the more substantial your construction will be. Generally, ¾-inch plywood is used for cabinetwork or flooring.

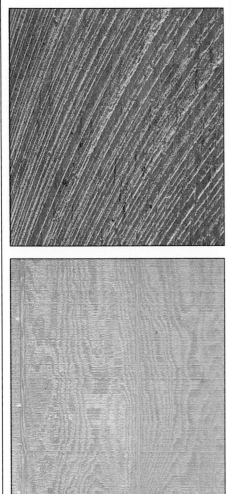

Top: *Close-up of rough-sawn board shows texture of rough lumber.*

Bottom: *Textured plywood siding looks at home in the garden, and doesn't show minor flaws and scratches.*

Estimating and Ordering

If you are planning a fairly simple project, such as a shed or playhouse, the best way to estimate your needs is to simply measure and count all the pieces from your plans. On architectural drawings for larger projects, a lumber list should be included.

If you have a problem estimating your lumber needs, ask the salespeople at the lumberyard to work them out for you.

Lumber is sold either by the lineal foot or by the board foot. The shorter lengths of finish wood are usually sold by the lineal or running foot, regardless of size. Lumber sold in large volume is almost always sold by the board foot.

A board foot is 1 inch thick, 12 inches wide, and 12 inches long. If you cut that board in half and stack it to make a 2 by 6 that is 12 inches long, you still have a board foot.

Lumber prices are often stated in dollars per thousand board feet.

To calculate the number of board feet of lumber you will need for your project, use this formula:

Thickness (in.) x Width (in.) x Length (ft.) divided by 12 = board feet, or

$$\frac{T'' \times W'' \times L'}{12} = \text{board feet}$$

Example: How many board feet are in an 8-foot-long 2 by 4 (written at the lumberyard as 2x4x8)?

Answer: 2 x 4 x 8 = 64, divided by 12 = 5.33 board feet.

When calculating board feet, always use the nominal rather than the actual size of lumber.

When you are ready to purchase a large amount of lumber, such as the lumber for a deck, call several yards and compare prices by asking what they charge per thousand for the type of lumber you need.

Alternatively, you can submit complete building supply lists to a number of suppliers and ask them to give you a bid. You will be surprised at the variations.

Woodworking Tools

Most experienced carpenters have a large variety of tools, primarily because these tools make their work much easier and faster. But you would be surprised what you can build with just a hand saw, hammer, level, tape measure, and square. In fact, with just these tools, you could build a house!

Life is much easier with a circular saw, though, so it has become a basic construction tool. Some of the basic tools considered essential for construction projects are shown on the opposite page.

Types of Saw Cuts and Joints

Sawing is probably the most basic skill required of anyone working with wood. The degree of precision you achieve with a saw can make the difference between shoddy and excellent work. If you know how to make the basic cuts with each of the many types of saws, you are well on your way to expertise.

Basic Saw Cuts

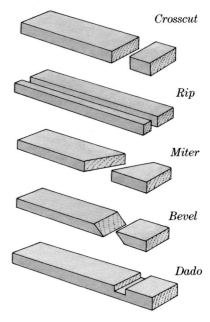

Crosscut

Rip

Miter

Bevel

Dado

Construction Tools

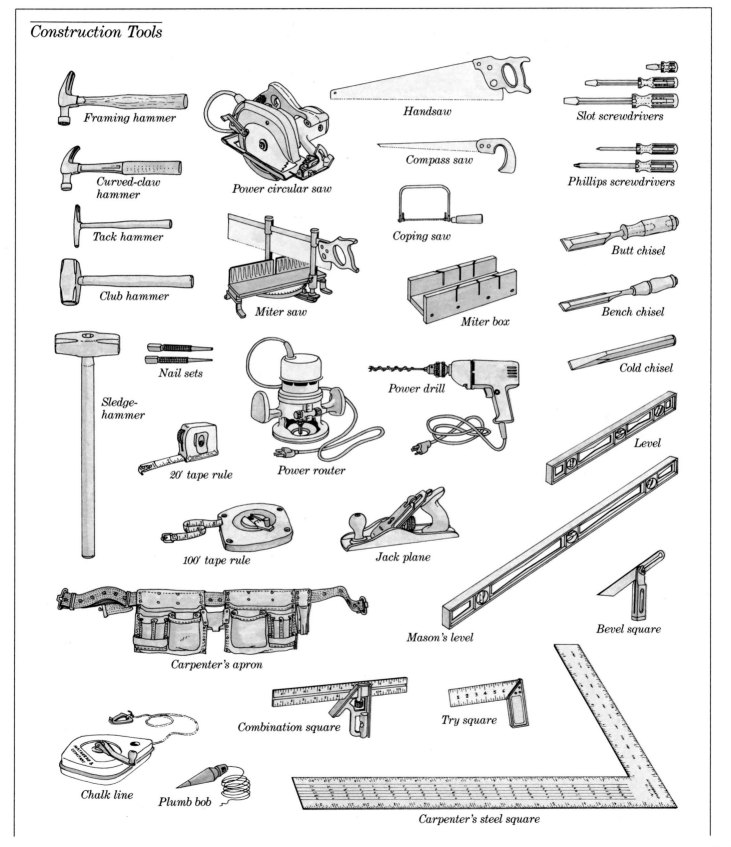

Framing hammer

Curved-claw hammer

Tack hammer

Club hammer

Sledge-hammer

Nail sets

20' tape rule

100' tape rule

Carpenter's apron

Chalk line

Plumb bob

Power circular saw

Miter saw

Power router

Combination square

Handsaw

Compass saw

Coping saw

Miter box

Power drill

Jack plane

Try square

Slot screwdrivers

Phillips screwdrivers

Butt chisel

Bench chisel

Cold chisel

Level

Mason's level

Bevel square

Carpenter's steel square

The basic cuts are actually quite simple. Depending on the project requirements, you can cut with the grain (rip cut) or across it (crosscut) or at an angle (miter or belvel cut). You can also cut all the way through the wood or only partially (as in a dado). The next section outlines the basic wood joints that can be made using these basic saw cuts.

Many ingenious methods of joining two pieces of wood together have been devised over the years. Making a good wood joint requires skill and patience, but the results are worth it; the joint is both strong and beautiful.

Butt Joint

This is a simple and commonly used joint, but one with relatively little strength. When joining a butt end to a board face, cut the butt end perfectly square so it will fit smooth and tight against the other board.

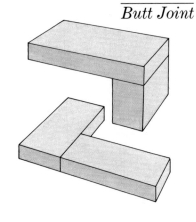

Butt Joint

Doweled Joints

If you plan to make numerous doweled joints, consider buying a doweling jig. It usually comes with complete instructions and will allow you to do very precise work.

Use at least two dowels on any joint. In order to join two pieces of wood together smoothly, the dowel holes must be drilled in precise locations for a perfect match. Bevel the end of the dowel slightly with a file so it will start into the hole smoothly, without splintering. The dowel must also be scored one or more times to allow air and excess glue to escape.

Squirt glue into the hole and then tap the dowel all the way in.

Doweled Joint

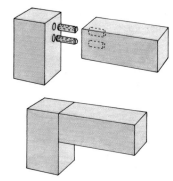

Miter Joint

This joint consists of two pieces of wood, generally cut at 45-degree angles, that fit together to form a right angle. A miter joint is commonly used for picture frames, molding, and fine cabinet work. You may wish to use a miter box rather than cutting free-hand. The miter box can be either an inexpensive wooden one or a more elaborate metal one that adjusts to cut various angles.

The two pieces of mitered wood can be joined in several ways. The simplest (and weakest) way is to glue both faces, clamp them together, and drive two corrugated fasteners across the joint on each side. More strength is gained by using glue and nailing or screwing the two pieces together. For a more professional appearance, put them together with dowels.

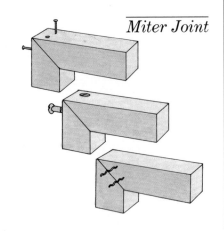

Miter Joint

Full-Lap Joint

This is a fairly simple but strong and attractive joint. The chief consideration here is that the board you cut must not be notched more than one-third its thickness; otherwise it will be too weak. To make the joint, cut the sides of the notch and then use a chisel to break out the piece. Put the lapping board in the notch and fasten, usually with glue and screws.

Full-Lap Joint

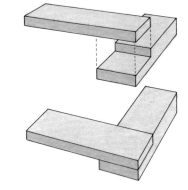

Half-Lap Joint

This is similar to the full-lap joint, but a shallower notch is required because you also notch the lapping board. Cut the crossboard notch. Then cut the lapping board notch. Fasten together with glue and screws.

Half-laps are very effective for joining boards in the middle, at right angles on the ends, or as an extension of each other. The latter use is appropriate when two large beams must meet over a supporting post.

Half-Lap Joint

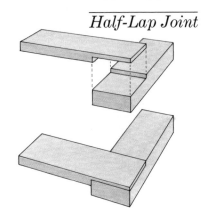

Plain Dado Joint

Dado joints are used to set the butt end of one board into the middle of another to provide support. The depth of the cut should be no more than one-third the thickness of the board. Chisel out the dado, starting from one edge, and work up toward the center of the board. Repeat for the other edge and dispose of waste.

Plain Dado Joint

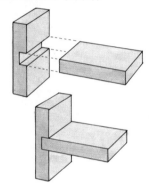

Stopped Dado Joint

The stopped dado joint is frequently used for shelves so the joint isn't seen from the front. It is easily done with a router or you can use a handsaw.

The dado stops a short distance from one edge of the board. To make room for a handsaw, chisel out a small section near the stop. Saw this piece to the proper depth and chisel out the waste wood. Cut a notch in the end of the cross-member. Apply glue to the end of the cross-member and slip it into place.

Stopped Dado Joint

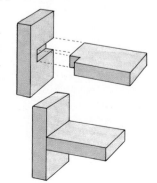

Rabbet Joint

An excellent choice for making drawers, this joint is easy to make and provides a finished appearance. Basically, it is a half-lap in one board that fits over the butt end of another. The rabbet cut should be no deeper than three-quarters the thickness of the board. Put the boards together with glue and finishing nails or screws.

Rabbet Joint

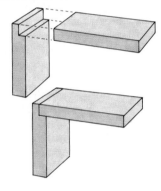

Mortise and Tenon Joint

This joint, commonly used in making furniture, is nearly invisible. Make the tenon first; fit the mortise to the tenon. Place the board for the tenon in a vise, butt end up, and make two vertical cuts with a backsaw. With the board on your workbench, cut the board faces. Make the mortise with a chisel or by drilling a series of holes. The bit should be $1/16$ inch smaller in diameter than the opening. Apply glue to the butt end and sides of the tenon and tap it into the mortise.

Mortise-and-Tenon Joint

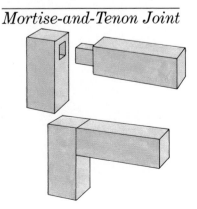

Wood Fasteners

If you are building a simple project like a raised planter bed, you can simply nail the boards together. But they will hold better if they are screwed together. Boards that are bolted together hold even better. Boards, beams, and posts can be supported or tied together with an amazing variety of devices. Below are some of the most common fasteners.

Wood Fasteners

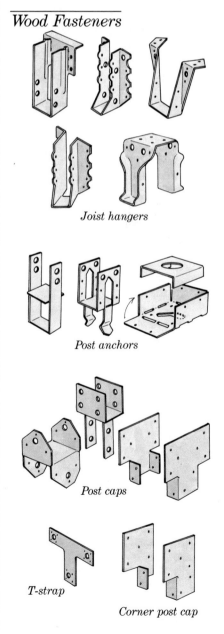

Joist hangers

Post anchors

Post caps

T-strap

Corner post cap

TECHNIQUES WITH BRICK

When you first look at the array of bricks offered by your local brickyard, the choices may overwhelm you. But once you have become acquainted with the basic types and qualities of brick, you will be able to approach the brickyard with authority.

The most common types of brick are building brick, paving brick, firebrick, and facing brick. For outdoor projects, it is unlikely that you will use facing brick, which is a high-priced brick of even color and texture used for covering a wall with a formal pattern. Firebrick, which is easily identifiable by its yellow color, is made with a special clay and fired at extremely high temperatures to make it hard and durable. In garden construction, it is used almost exclusively for lining barbecues and fire pits.

Building brick is the basic brick used in garden construction. Some building bricks have a rough finish, which makes them excellent for walks and patios, while others have a smooth finish, making them more suitable for use indoors or under protective cover, since smooth bricks may be quite slippery when wet.

Building bricks are divided into three grades of hardness to withstand different degrees of exposure to the elements. These are: SW (severe weathering), MW (moderate weathering), and NW (no weathering). SW bricks should be used outdoors where the bricks will be placed in direct contact with the ground, or in any area that experiences sub-zero winters. MW bricks can be used in areas that are exposed to sub-freezing temperatures. Limit NW bricks to indoor or fully protected areas.

Paving bricks are similar to building bricks, but are much harder so they will not break under heavy traffic. Paving bricks are also slightly larger and more exact in their dimensions than building brick. They are designed for use without mortar and make an excellent choice for brick-on-sand projects, such as patios, walks, and driveways.

Of Bricks and Mortar

Bricks are made in increments of 4 inches and referred to by their nominal dimensions rather than exact sizes. Standard bricks are nominally 4 inches wide and 8 inches long, but are actually 3⅝ inches wide and 7⅝ inches long to allow space for a ⅜-inch-thick joint.

When you calculate the number of bricks needed for a patio or path, first determine how many square feet must be covered. For square or rectangular patios or walks, you can find the total square feet by multiplying length times width. For patios with circular outlines multiply 3.14 times the radius squared. For irregular outlines, draw the shape on graph paper with each square equal to one square foot—count all the squares that are over half within the area to estimate the square footage. For standard-sized bricks placed flat side up, allow five bricks per square foot, then add five percent to the total to allow for breakage.

When estimating the number of bricks needed for a wall, you again find the square footage by multiplying length times width. Then, for a single-thickness wall, allow seven standard-sized bricks per square foot. If the wall is two bricks thick, as many are, allow 14 bricks per square foot. Brick walls sometimes have a brick cap, often with the bricks laid side by side. To calculate the number of bricks needed for the cap, divide the length of the wall by 4 inches, which is equal to the width of a brick.

Mortar

Mortar is a mixture of cement, lime, sand, and water. Unless you are fitting bricks together in the brick-on-sand method, you will need mortar to keep them in place.

Visit a brickyard to select the right shape, size, color, and texture of brick.

There are several types of mortar, to suit different needs. For small jobs, you may want to use premixed mortar. You can lay about 40 bricks with one bag of premixed mortar and water. Another choice is masonry cement, which is already mixed with lime. With one bag of masonry cement, plus sand and water, you can lay about 100 bricks.

For larger jobs, buy the ingredients separately and mix your own mortar. A good all-purpose mix is made with one part cement, one part lime, and six parts sand. Mix these together by the shovelful in a wheelbarrow before adding water. (Watch that you don't put more sand on your shovel than cement, which is a common error.) Once the elements are thoroughly mixed, add water, a little at a time. When the water level is correct, the mortar should be plastic, or easily molded, and should stand up by itself in little waves without being crumbly (too dry) or sinking immediately (too wet). The exact amount of water to be added varies with each mix, depending on how wet the sand is.

Patterns

Give thought to the pattern you want before you start a patio or walk. Some patterns are more complicated than others, and require more time and more bricks, but the end result may be spectacular. Since your patio or pathway is going to be around for a long time, take the time to do it right.

Bricks can be laid in several basic patterns and can be altered and combined to produce a vast array of individual effects. The common brick patterns shown here are widely used and quite simple to lay. Only the diagonal herringbone may present some complications because of numerous cuts that must be made along the edges.

If you want to combine several patterns, or create your own pattern, sketch it first to visualize the overall effect. Combined patterns, or very complicated ones, may confuse the eye. Whatever pattern you choose, keep it balanced and symmetrical.

Brick Patio Patterns

Traditional

Ladder weave

Jack-on-jack

Basket weave

Half-basket weave

Basket weave variation

Pinwheel

Whorling square

Concentric squares

Herringbone

Diagonal herringbone

Circular

Brick Walk Patterns

Traditional

Jack-on-jack

Geometrical

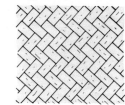

Bias with border

Basket weave with grass

Curved path

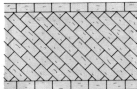

Brick Tools

A lot of brickwork can be done with just a few basic tools; you probably have some of them already. A trowel, level, and hammer are all you really need to build a small brick planter or lay a brick sidewalk. But having the right tools can make your work a lot easier. The tools shown, none of which is particularly expensive, are considered the basics.

Brick Tools

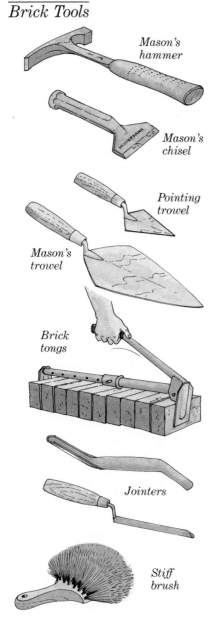

Mason's hammer

Mason's chisel

Pointing trowel

Mason's trowel

Brick tongs

Jointers

Stiff brush

How to Cut Brick

Place the brick on a bed of sand or dirt, not on concrete. Turn the brick set so the beveled edge is facing toward the waste end of the brick.

Score the brick lightly on all four sides with a series of light taps. Place the tip of the brick set on the line and give it a sharp rap with the hammer.

Clean up any ragged edges—there will be lots—with the brick set or the cutting end of a brick hammer.

Note that the cut does not have to be perfectly vertical; you can place the cut end down in the mortar and it will never be seen.

If you plan to cut a lot of brick for a patio or walk, or want particularly clean lines on a large project, you may want to cut the brick with a saw. This can be done with an abrasive blade in a circular saw.

Whether you use a brick set or a saw, always wear goggles when cutting brick to protect your eyes from the sharp chunks and slivers that split off during the process.

Laying Brick

Methods of laying brick range from the simple to the very complex, but all styles can be laid by a determined worker. Remember that the result doesn't have to be absolutely perfect;

imperfections give brickwork that rustic touch. Indeed, a professional may put some bricks slightly out of line just to achieve that look.

Brick-on-sand. This is the easiest method, and requires only that there be a permanent edging around the perimeter to hold the bricks in place, and that they be bedded on 2 inches of level sand.

First outline the area by driving stakes at the four corners and connecting them with string. Remove all sod and soil within the area to a depth of about 4½ inches—the thickness of a brick plus 2 inches of sand.

To keep weeds and grass from growing up through the bricks, spray the area with a grass retardant or cover it with black plastic. If you use plastic, punch numerous holes in it for drainage.

If you are laying the patio or walkway on fill dirt, which may be loose and soft, pack it first so the ground and bricks will settle evenly.

Once the area is cleared and prepared, you are ready to install the edging. Lay a test pattern from one side of the patio or walk to the other, then fit the edging to the bricks. This is easier and more foolproof than calculating the number of bricks that will fit within a border.

Cutting Brick

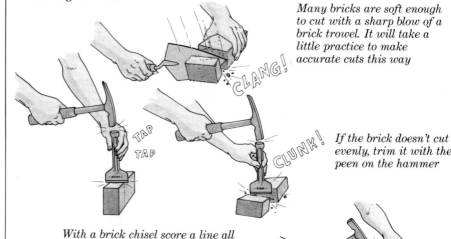

Many bricks are soft enough to cut with a sharp blow of a brick trowel. It will take a little practice to make accurate cuts this way

CLANG!

TAP TAP

CLUNK!

If the brick doesn't cut evenly, trim it with the peen on the hammer

With a brick chisel score a line all around the brick where you want it cut—then sever it with a sharp blow

TINK!

The edging should be flush with the surface of the surrounding lawn so that a mower can be run over it. The edging can be an elaborate one, such as brick set in concrete, or it can be something simple, like old railroad ties or 2 by 4s of decay-resistant wood. When laying 2-by-4 edging, use a stretched string, staked in place, to make sure the edging is straight. After the edging is secure, cut off the stakes below the surface of the edging.

Fill the edged area with a 2-inch layer of sand, and spread the sand with a flat-bottomed shovel. Spray the sand until it is thoroughly damp. Then smooth and level it precisely with a screed—a straight 2 by 4 cut to fit inside the edging, with the ends notched so that 2½ inches of board extends below the edging. The notched ears ride on the edging and smooth the sand below.

After the sand has been smoothed, start laying bricks from one corner, working out in the desired pattern. Press the bricks firmly into the sand, and keep each one tight against the other. As you progress, kneel on a piece of plywood to better distribute your weight and avoid disturbing the sand base.

Check regularly, using a level or straight 2 by 4, that the tops of the bricks are flush with one another. If one is low, take it out and add sand; if one is high, remove some sand.

When all the bricks are in place, cover them with about ¼ inch of sand. Let the sand dry, then sweep it back and forth. The sand will fall into the cracks between the bricks and, like tiny wedges, lock each brick in place. Leave the sand on the bricks for a few days while you walk on your new path, then sweep some more to complete the process.

Bricks in Dry Mortar
Many people prefer to have a mortar joint between bricks, which gives them a more finished appearance. An easy way to add a mortar joint is to sweep in dry mortar.

Laying Bricks on Sand

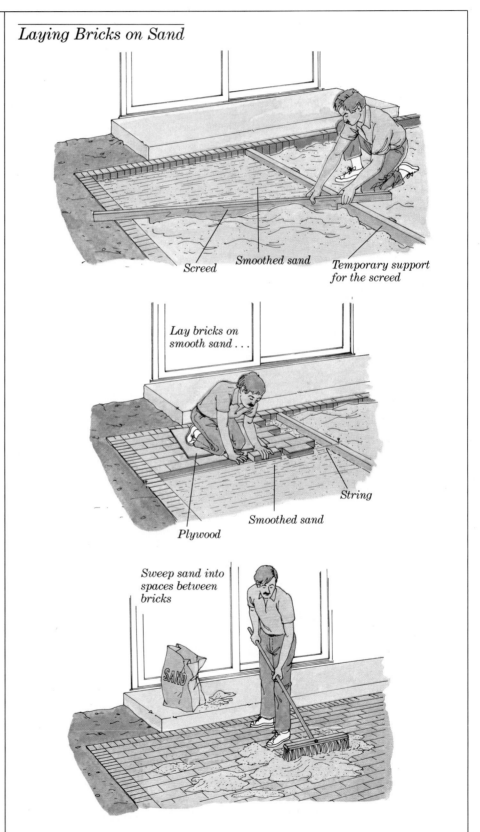

Screed   Smoothed sand   Temporary support for the screed

Lay bricks on smooth sand . . .

String

Smoothed sand

Plywood

Sweep sand into spaces between bricks

SAND

If the bricks are going to be walked on, rather than being strictly ornamental, they must be set on a firm surface, such as a concrete slab. If placed on sand, they will shift slightly with pressure, causing the the mortar joint to crack.

To lay bricks with dry mortar, set them in the desired pattern, spacing them ⅜ inch apart. Use lengths of ⅜-inch plywood, or the tip of your little finger, to set the spacing.

Mix one part of masonry cement to three parts of dry sand, then sweep the mixture over the bricks until all the joints are filled. Take your time to sweep each brick as clean as possible to minimize stains in the next step.

Now, with a hose nozzle set on fine mist, spray the entire area. The water must penetrate all the mortar. Wait 15 minutes and repeat to make sure that the mortar is thoroughly saturated.

By the time the bricks dry, the mortar probably will have settled. Sweep in another layer of dry mortar, filling all the joints, and repeat the fine watering to finish the job.

Bricks in Wet Mortar
This is the most professional way to set bricks, but it requires some skill and patience. Bricks set in wet mortar must be laid on a concrete base to prevent shifting.

Laying Bricks in Dry Mortar

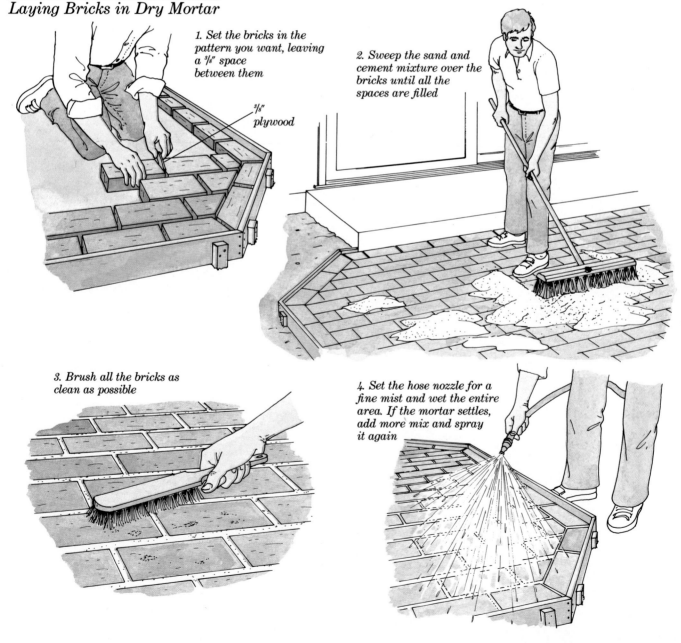

1. Set the bricks in the pattern you want, leaving a ⅜" space between them

⅜" plywood

2. Sweep the sand and cement mixture over the bricks until all the spaces are filled

3. Brush all the bricks as clean as possible

4. Set the hose nozzle for a fine mist and wet the entire area. If the mortar settles, add more mix and spray it again

If you already have a sidewalk or concrete patio, you can lay bricks directly on the existing surface. Work only in an area that can be covered in about two hours—before the mortar becomes too stiff to work.

Begin by laying the edging. Wet the concrete slab, then trowel on mortar about ¾-inch to 1-inch thick and place the first brick. Press it firmly into the mortar until it rests on just ½ inch of mortar. Apply mortar to the edge of the next brick and press the mortared side firmly in place against the first one. There should be just ⅜-inch of mortar between the two bricks. Use a trowel to scrape up any excess mortar. Rap each brick with the butt of the trowel handle to set it.

Continue working in this manner along the edging. Once the border is complete, begin working toward the center. Spread a 1-inch layer of mortar over a section large enough to hold about 12 bricks, then mortar the brick edges and put them in place.

When the mortar has set up to the point where the firm pressure of your thumb leaves only a print, it is time to finish with a jointer. Press the mortar firmly, smoothing it until it is flush with, or just below, the brick surface.

Keep the mortar continuously damp for three or four days to prevent cracking as it dries.

Laying Bricks in Wet Mortar

1. Lay some bricks on the base concrete in the desired pattern to see if they fit and look the way you want

Concrete base

⅜″ space between bricks

2. Butter the end of the edging bricks and put them in place on both edges of the project

3. Butter the end and side of each brick and fill in the area between the edging bricks

4. Swipe off the squished-out mortar with your trowel, then use a jointer to press and smooth the joints

TECHNIQUES WITH STONE

*S*tonemasonry requires great patience and a certain artistic flair in finding and fitting just the right stone. You can work at your own pace and quit the job at any stage when you have had enough for one day.

Working with stone involves finding the right type of stone, cutting the stone to the needed size, and laying the stone to form a patio or a wall. Some projects, like a dry stone wall, do not even require the use of mortar to hold the stones in place.

Types of Stone

Stone for yard and garden work falls into two basic categories. Become familiar with each type so you can choose the most appropriate for your project and your pocketbook.

Quarried Stone

Quarried stone, such as flagstone, is found naturally in many parts of the country, but is generally purchased for yard use. It is excellent for use in patios, walks, or stepping stones.

Fieldstone

Fieldstone is just natural stone found in fields or along streams and rivers. When buying or hunting for fieldstone, be sure to look for the flattest possible stones, because round ones are much more difficult to work with.

Roughly-squared stone is fieldstone, too, but the irregular edges have been chiseled off. This labor raises the price, and it is something you can do yourself.

Estimating and Ordering

Because the sizes of stones are so varied, the best way to "estimate" how much you will need, if you are hauling your own rock, is to build as you haul, and stop when you have enough. If you are buying the stone, let the supplier make the calculations for you, based on the square footage.

How to Cut Stone

Cutting stone is easier than you might imagine. The basic tools are a pitching chisel and a pointing chisel, a 2½-pound or 5-pound hammer, and protective eyewear.

Place the rock on a bed of sand. (Placing it on concrete will cause the rock to break from shock in the wrong place.) Turn the rock and look for existing cracks or a defined grain on which to make the split. Score the line to be cut by making a series of small cuts with the chisel, then place the chisel on the line and give it one or two sharp raps. Trim any uneven surfaces with the hammer and chisel.

Cutting Stone

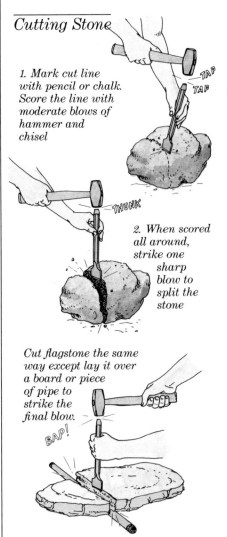

1. Mark cut line with pencil or chalk. Score the line with moderate blows of hammer and chisel

TAP
TAP

THUNK

2. When scored all around, strike one sharp blow to split the stone

Cut flagstone the same way except lay it over a board or piece of pipe to strike the final blow.

BAP!

Stones are full of character and are individually unique.

Laying Flagstone Walks and Patios

If you want to lay a natural-looking pathway, simply place the stones where you want them on the grass, spacing them so you can step comfortably. Remove the sod and enough dirt to set the flagstone flush with the surface, and bed each stone in some sand to keep it from rocking.

When flagstone is used to make a solid patio or walk, it must be mortared in place on a concrete slab. Dry mortaring is unsatisfactory because the flagstone will shift, with pressure, and crack the mortar joints.

Flagstone is set in mortar in much the same way as bricks are. Start by laying out the flagstones like a jigsaw puzzle to get the best fit, then bed the stones in about 2 inches of mortar on the concrete slab. Then, fill in the spaces with either a wet mortar or a dry mortar that you dampen with a fine spray.

Laying Stone Walls

Stone walls can be laid with or without mortar, but the stones must fit together so that one holds the other; you cannot rely on mortar to keep the stones in place.

A mortared stone wall must be supported by a concrete footing. If it isn't, movement due to frost heave will crack the joints.

Dry stone walls are normally laid wider at the base than at the top to minimize the chances of the top layer falling off. These walls can be markedly strengthened by mortaring the top stones in place.

Mortaring a wall takes a lot of mortar. After test-fitting a stone, lift it clear and fill the spot with a thick bed of mortar. Put the stone back in place and rap it sharply with the butt of the trowel handle to set it.

When the mortar is just hard enough to take a thumbprint, tool all the mortar joints by pressing them firmly with the back of a spoon or a convex jointer.

Laying Flagstone

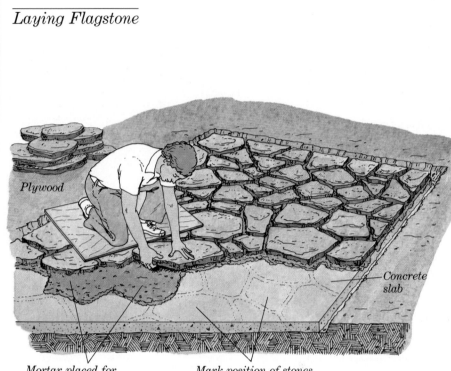

Plywood

Concrete slab

Mortar placed for 2 or 3 stones

Mark position of stones before placing mortar

Laying a Mortared Stone Wall

As you go along, dry-fit 2 or 3 stones at a time before you set them in the mortar

Stake

String with line level

TECHNIQUES WITH CONCRETE

Many concrete projects, such as sidewalks and patios, are within the realm of the do-it-yourselfer, so don't hesitate to consider a concrete project even if you have never worked with concrete before.

One of the first things to keep in mind is the difference between cement, concrete, and mortar. Concrete is made by mixing specific amounts of cement, sand, gravel, and water. Mortar is a mixture of cement, sand, and water—no gravel.

The most common type of cement is portland cement. Cement is a dry powder mixture of lime, clay, and gypsum. When it is mixed with water, a chemical reaction occurs that causes it to harden.

The sand and gravel that are added to a concrete mix are known as aggregates. Sand is a fine aggregate. Gravel is a coarse aggregate. Water is the catalyst that causes the cement to harden and bind to the aggregates. Whether you mix your own concrete or order it delivered usually depends on the size of the job. It is much cheaper to mix your own, but in many cases it is not practical. Even using a cement mixer, for instance, it would take days to mix and pour the slab for a two-car garage. If you order the concrete delivered, on the other hand, the job can be done in two or three hours.

For very small jobs, you can buy ready-mixed concrete, to which you just add water. For medium-sized jobs, you can mix your own concrete in a wheelbarrow or in a rented concrete mixer. In many areas, concrete is sold by the trailerful, so you can haul it yourself.

Laying concrete is heavy work. Arrange to have some friends help you.

If your project calls for more than two cubic yards of concrete, consider ordering it. Concrete delivered in a truck will cost between $55 and $70 per cubic yard (plus any extra charges if the delivery people have to wait long at your site).

Estimating Materials

Concrete is normally estimated in cubic yards. To calculate your needs, use this formula:

Thickness (in.) x Length (ft.) x Width (ft.) divided by 12 = cubic feet. Divide this by 27 for the number of cubic yards. It is a good idea to always order 10 percent more than you need. The chart on this page will speed up your calculations.

Placing an Order

When ordering mixed concrete, you will need to know how rich a mix you need. After you tell the supplier how many yards you need, you will be asked: "What sack mix do you want?" Translated, that means: How many sacks of cement do you want put into each cubic yard of concrete? Five-sack mixes are used for patios and sidewalks, and stronger six-sack mixes are used for driveways and garage floors.

If you are building in an inaccessible area, such as on a slope or across a wet lawn where a truck cannot pass, the concrete can be pumped from the truck to your site.

Calculating Volume of Concrete

Find the point where a vertical line from the number of square feet you have crosses the red line for the thickness you want. From there, follow a horizontal line to the scale at the right to find the amount of concrete you will need.

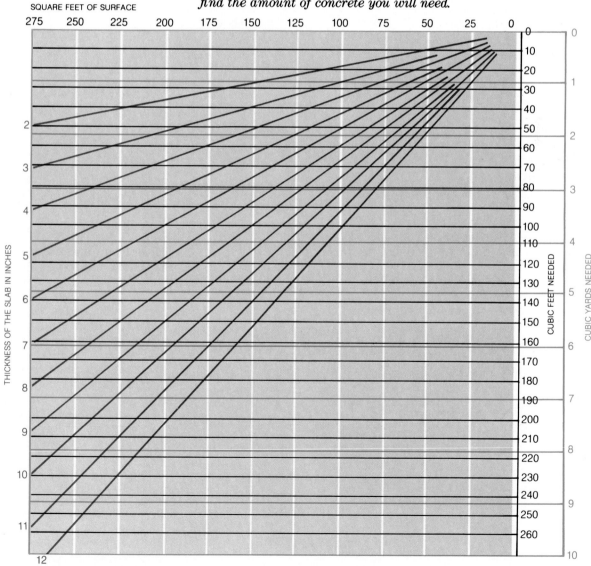

Mixing Your Own

Concrete is a mixture of portland cement, sand (fine aggregates), gravel (coarse aggregates), and water. A standard mix for home construction is made with one part cement, two parts sand, and three parts gravel. These should all be placed in a wheelbarrow and mixed together with a flat bottomed shovel or a hoe.

After the dry ingredients are mixed, water is added. The amount of water depends on how wet your sand is. Add the water slowly and keep mixing, making sure to turn the dry ingredients on the bottom of the wheelbarrow. The end result should be a plastic, or easily molded, mix that is neither crumbly (too dry) nor soupy (too wet).

Add less water than you think is needed to your first few batches or the mixture might end up too soupy. If you do add too much water, add some more cement and aggregates, in proportion, and mix thoroughly.

Pouring a Slab

Pouring a concrete slab for a patio, sidewalk, or even a driveway, is not particularly complicated. All you need to do is follow the steps below.

Laying Out the Site

The first step in pouring a patio or sidewalk is to lay out the site. For a patio, this is done by simply driving stakes at the corners and stretching string between them. For sidewalks, drive stakes along the edge and run a string between them, checking to make sure the strings are parallel. Curved edges can be laid out using a garden hose to mark the borders.

If you want the slab to be flush with the ground, excavate the area to a depth of 3½ inches. This is the thickness of a 2 by 4, which is the standard material used for concrete forms. Wherever you have curves, stake redwood bender board or plastic lawn edging in place.

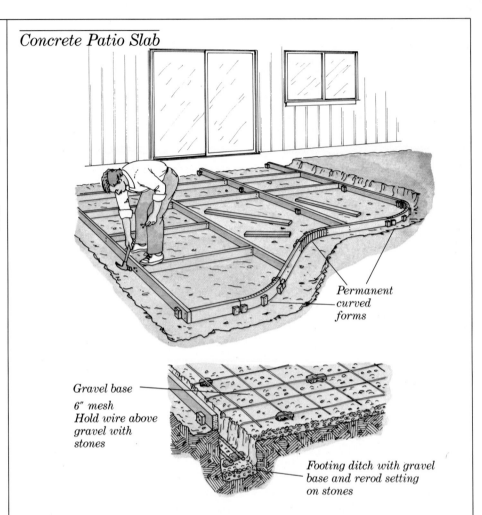

Concrete Patio Slab

Permanent curved forms

Gravel base
6" mesh
Hold wire above gravel with stones

Footing ditch with gravel base and rerod setting on stones

After the excavation, lay the forms and hold them in place with 2 by 2 stakes driven every 4 feet on the outside of the forms. Nail the stakes to the form boards. Check that the stakes are below the tops of the forms.

Laying concrete in large areas can be made a more manageable job by sectioning the area to be covered into smaller areas with 2 by 4 dividers. Nail the ends of the dividers to the outside forms and support the middle with stakes that are cut off 2 inches below the top of the board so they will be covered with concrete.

Unless protected, these permanent divider forms will be stained and marred when the concrete is poured. To prevent this, cover the tops with masking tape, which can be removed after the concrete has set.

Handling Concrete

Spreading and smoothing the concrete is the most important step in the process. Try to have lots of helpers on hand for this step so that no time is wasted, especially in hot weather, when concrete dries quickly.

Take the following steps when the truck backs up and is ready to pour:

1. Start at the farthest spot from the truck; keep the chute moving so concrete doesn't pile up in one area.

2. Have helpers spread and work the concrete as it is being dumped; they should shovel concrete from high areas into low areas.

3. Once one section has been filled, other helpers should level it with a screed. Place a long board on top of the forms and "saw" it back and forth to level the concrete.

4. Floating is the next step. For patios or driveways, use a *bull float,* a long-handled float that smooths the concrete. For sidewalks, do the same with a wooden hand float.

5. Troweling is the final finishing step. Use a wooden float for a non-skid finish, and steel trowels for a slick finish. Start finish troweling when the film of water has disappeared off the concrete. Kneel on pieces of plywood to disburse your weight as you work backwards.

6. Curing concrete is critical. It must be kept continuously wet for four to six days. Since you can't spray it all the time, you can cover it with rags and soak them. The best way, however, is to soak the surface, then cover it with a layer of plastic film and weight the edges of the film. This traps all the moisture inside.

Disguising Concrete

Concrete can be finished in many ways; in fact, some disguises are so artful that you may not even realize it is concrete at first. Several of these attractive finishes are discussed here.

Patterned Concrete

A blank expanse of concrete can be made more interesting by adding patterns. One simple method is to texture it by using a push broom on fresh concrete. Just pull the broom over the concrete, letting the bristles create a patterned, nonskid surface. You can use wavy, angled, or straight strokes for the pattern.

A wavy broom finish adds interest and increases traction.

Finishing Concrete

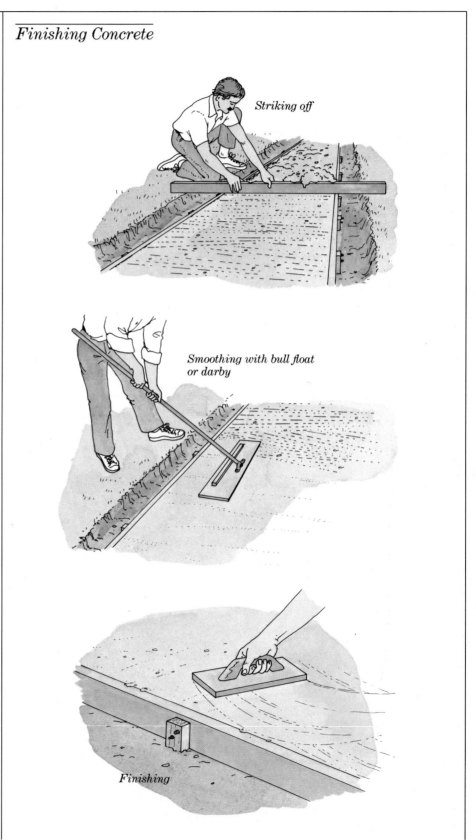

Striking off

Smoothing with bull float or darby

Finishing

91

An equally easy way to create a pattern is by sprinkling rock salt over concrete that has just been finish floated with a trowel. Afterwards, lightly float the concrete again to press the salt below the surface. When the salt melts, it will leave a pitted surface. This method is not recommended for areas that have freezing winters.

Imaginative designs can be added by pressing leaves along the edge of a concrete patio or walk; these impressions bear an interesting resemblance to fossil remains when they are dry. Ring patterns can be made with different-sized tin cans, and wooden letters or numbers, available at most hardware stores, can be used to personalize your patio or create an intriguing design.

Concrete can also be patterned to look like flagstone. This is done with a jointing tool, or a piece of ½-inch copper pipe bent into an elongated S-shape. Use one end of the tool to groove the concrete in the approximate outlines of a flagstone surface.

Make large "flagstones" for large areas, smaller ones for sidewalks. The tooling must be done twice, once after the concrete has been bull floated, the second time after it has been finish floated.

Finally, concrete can be patterned with a rented steel stamping tool. The base of the tool has replaceable patterns that resemble, for instance, brick or cobblestone. It is pressed into the surface while the concrete is still fresh to form the patterns.

Exposed-Aggregate Surface

Exposed-aggregate concrete, in which the top is coated with attractive small stones, has long been a popular style. Its quality is directly related to the beauty of the stones. Choose them carefully for texture and color.

To create an exposed-aggregate surface, first divide the area to be covered into smaller segments so the concrete will not harden before you finish. Immediately after an area has been bull floated, sprinkle the stones on evenly. With a helper, use flat shovels or a long 2 by 4 to press the stones firmly in the concrete. If necessary, run a wood float over the stones until you can just see the tops.

When the surface has fully hardened—usually three to five hours—use a hose and push broom to sweep away the top thin layer of concrete and expose the stones. Be careful that neither the broom nor the hose breaks the stones loose. After the initial cleaning, let the stones dry for another hour, then go over the surface lightly again with water and a broom to remove the concrete film.

Top: A sprinkling of rock salt creates a pitted surface.

Bottom: *Expose aggregate with a broom and water.*

Patterned Concrete

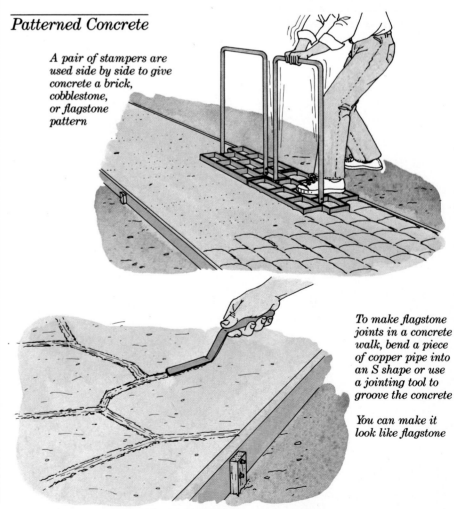

A pair of stampers are used side by side to give concrete a brick, cobblestone, or flagstone pattern

To make flagstone joints in a concrete walk, bend a piece of copper pipe into an S shape or use a jointing tool to groove the concrete

You can make it look like flagstone

Concrete need not be boring. On the contrary, it has the ability to take on any shape and it fits with virtually any landscape style.

Colored Finish

Concrete can be colored in three basic ways:

One way is to simply stain or paint the concrete, using stains or paints specifically made for this purpose. These should only be applied to concrete that is at least one year old; even then, foot traffic will soon wear the covering thin.

Another method is to sprinkle a coloring agent over the surface of freshly floated concrete. It is difficult to spread the agent really evenly, however, and the result often looks splotchy. If you try this method, put on the first coat of coloring agent, trowel it smooth, then fill in the pale areas with more coloring agent and trowel again.

The best way to color concrete is to add the coloring agent to the entire concrete mix, either in a mixer or in a wheelbarrow. For large jobs this can be quite expensive, though, so you may want to use colored concrete for only the final 1-inch top layer.

Add color to stamped concrete for a special effect.

Index

Conversion Chart

U.S. Measure and Metric Measure Conversion Chart

	Symbol	When you know:	Multiply by	To find:			
		Formulas for Exact Measures			**Rounded Measures for Quick Reference**		
Mass (Weight)	oz	ounces	28.35	grams	1 oz		= 30 g
	lb	pounds	0.45	kilograms	4 oz		= 115 g
	g	grams	0.035	ounces	8 oz		= 225 g
	kg	kilograms	2.2	pounds	16 oz	= 1 lb	= 450 kg
					32 oz	= 2 lb	= 900 kg
					36 oz	= 2 1/4 lb	= 1000g (a kg)
Volume	tsp	teaspoons	5.0	milliliters	1/4 tsp	= 1/24 oz	= 1 ml
	tbsp	tablespoons	15.0	milliliters	1/2 tsp	= 1/12 oz	= 2 ml
	fl oz	fluid ounces	29.57	milliliters	1 tsp	= 1/6 oz	= 5 ml
	c	cups	0.24	liters	1 tbsp	= 1/2 oz	= 15 ml
	pt	pints	0.47	liters	1 c	= 8 oz	= 250 ml
	qt	quarts	0.95	liters	2 c (1 pt)	= 16 oz	= 500 ml
	gal	gallons	3.785	liters	4 c (1 qt)	= 32 oz	= 1 l
	ml	milliliters	0.034	fluid ounces	4 qt (1 gal)	= 128 oz	= 3 3/4 l
Length	in.	inches	2.54	centimeters	3/8 in.	= 1 cm	
	ft	feet	30.48	centimeters	1 in.	= 2.5 cm	
	yd	yards	0.9144	meters	2 in.	= 5 cm	
	mi	miles	1.609	kilometers	2-1/2 in.	= 6.5 cm	
	km	kilometers	0.621	miles	12 in. (1 ft)	= 30 cm	
	m	meters	1.094	yards	1 yd	= 90 cm	
	cm	centimeters	0.39	inches	100 ft	= 30 m	
					1 mi	= 1.6 km	
Temperature	°F	Fahrenheit	5/9 (after subtracting 32)	Celsius	32°F	= 0°C	
					68°F	= 20°C	
	°C	Celsius	9/5 (then add 32)	Fahrenheit	212°F	= 100°C	
Area	in.^{2}	square inches	6.452	square centimeters	1 in.^{2}	= 6.5 cm^2	
	ft^2	square feet	929.0	square centimeters	1 ft^2	= 930 cm^2	
	yd^2	square yards	8361.0	square centimeters	1 yd^2	= 8360 cm^2	
	a	acres	0.4047	hectares	1 a	= 4050 m^2	